PROMISE OR PRETENCE?

A Christian's Guide to Sexual Morals

A. E. Harvey

SCM PRESS LTD

*Unless otherwise stated, biblical quotations are taken
from the Revised English Bible*

0 334 01283 X

First published 1994
by SCM Press Ltd
26–30 Tottenham Road, London N1 4BZ

Typeset at The Spartan Press Ltd,
Lymington, Hants
and printed in Great Britain by
Biddles Ltd, Guildford and King's Lynn

Contents

Preface

At the end of August 1993 the first of two articles which I had written on 'Marriage, Sex and the Bible' were published in the journal *Theology*. This caught the attention of the national and even the international press, and provoked a startling volume of comment and correspondence – which was a sign, not of any great originality in what I had written (most of it had been said, even if rather quietly, many times before), but of the extent to which people are still unaware both of the resources of the Christian faith in these matters and of the attitudes and procedures which are now officially authorized in the church. The moment seemed right to try to write a book which would place these issues before a wider public and suggest the grounds for hope and confidence which may be found in the Christian religion.

This is not a book on sex itself, but on Christian thinking about relationships in which sex is an important component (though in every case less important than love). I lay no claim to expert knowledge about these. My only qualifications are that I am a specialist in the New Testament and have some experience in applying Christian insights to contemporary problems. If there are facts or sensitivities that I have ignored, I shall gladly receive correction. My object has not been to cover the ground exhaustively but to suggest the methods by which any thinking Christian may bring the resources of the faith to bear on the contemporary situation. A more detailed account of my approach to the teaching of Jesus on this and other moral questions may be found in my book *Strenuous Commands: The Ethic of Jesus*, SCM Press and TPI 1990.

I owe a debt of gratitude to a number of friends and advisers: to Henry Harvey (a relative by marriage) who first urged me to write the book; to Jane Cooper, Sister Hilary Markey CSMV and Bernard Merry, all of whom read parts of the typescript and helped me with comments and encouragement; and above all to my wife and family, who for over thirty years have gently, humorously and affectionately helped me to acquire at least that minimum of understanding which is necessary if one is even to attempt to write about this sensitive but desperately important subject.

Westminster Abbey, January 1994 Anthony Harvey

I

Promise or Pretence?

Christianity – like many other religions – is about love. So is marriage. So is (or should be) family life. Yet, today, more and more marriages become loveless and end in divorce; marriage itself has to compete with widespread cohabitation; family loyalties disintegrate under new social and economic pressures; the sexual component in human relationships is exploited to an unprecedented degree; and young people receive little guidance in the direction of that fidelity and restraint which in the past has been thought a condition for a lasting and loving relationship. So what has the religion of love to say about all this? Can it not do something to strengthen the social institutions of marriage and family life and, with its long experience both of fulfilment and of failure, offer guidance and support to those who are sincerely seeking a lifelong relationship grounded in love?

To this, many Christians may feel they have a clear answer. The Bible, they say, sets clear standards. Jesus forbade divorce, and it is for the church to uphold this ideal in the lives of its members. Marriage is the only context in which a full sexual relationship is legitimate. By failing to proclaim these principles clearly and courageously, the church has contributed to the prevailing moral confusion. Any attempt to adjust them in the light of modern social conditions is a compromise with the spirit of the age. Christians are entrusted with a revelation of God's will for all men and women. This revelation embraces their family and sexual lives, and offers a firm basis on which to challenge the laxity and permissiveness which is undermining our social institutions today.

But others are not so sure. Does the Bible really speak so clearly? Certainly the Old Testament describes some outstandingly faithful couples and contains shining examples of happy and devoted married life. But it also has stories that are a great deal less edifying; it seems to condone polygamy; and its approach to the role of women in society is, to say the least, unenlightened. As to the New Testament, family relationships are defined in a firmly hierarchical mould. Jesus appears to talk with approval about 'hating one's father and one's mother'; and if Paul approves of marriage at all, it seems only because the alternative is something worse! The one really definite teaching is that about divorce; and this is so rigorous that for centuries Christian people have been searching for ways of coming to terms with it. So are Christians really in a position to give a lesson to the world about marriage and family life? If the heart of the Christian faith is love, is it not more 'Christian' to try to promote truly loving relationships within whatever forms or conventions are accepted by society at the present time?

The trouble is that in this matter no Christian church can afford to leave things open. Christians need to know where they stand, there have to be clear rules. If Jesus intended to set a high standard (as we shall see that he did), the churches cannot witness to it effectively if they allow their members to adopt any pattern of life they like. Every church has to uphold a rule – which means that it has to have a clear policy towards those who fail to conform to it. The historic churches have done this in different ways. The Church of Rome and the Church of England (along with some other Anglican churches) have adopted a particularly difficult régime. They have interpreted Jesus' teaching to mean that marriage is 'indissoluble'. This means that even if the couple are divorced their original marriage somehow persists, and makes it impossible for the church to accept a second marriage as proper or legitimate. They have also adhered officially to their traditional teaching that all sexual intercourse outside marriage is inherently sinful.

Now of course it can be argued that these churches are doing the right thing. In the face of an increasingly permissive and love-less society, the right strategy is to maintain absolute values. To lessen the challenge presented by the Christian religion is to compromise with a debased morality. The only way to preserve the institution of marriage as the church has received it is by insisting that it is a totally committed lifelong relationship which excludes all other sexual liaisons both before and after marriage. And indeed this is the teaching which most clergy feel bound to adhere to: marriage is for life, divorce is always sinful, re-marriage while the first spouse is alive is inadmissible and no sex is permitted before or outside marriage. But it cannot be denied that this involves a great deal of *pretence*.

Faced by a couple one or both of whom have remarried, a parish priest must either follow the rules, refuse to admit them to full membership and communion (however good 'Christians' they were before) and seek to persuade them to return to their original spouses (who by now may have re-married also!); or else he must pretend that the church welcomes them as they are and that he can even 'bless' their second marriage. Faced by a couple who come to him to be married but who have been living together for some time, he cannot legally refuse to marry them on these grounds. He could ask them to repent of their previous conduct; logically this means that one of them should move out so that they live separately until they are married. But since he is likely to want to encourage them in their decision to get married, the last thing he will try to do when he starts their marriage preparation is to give them a bad conscience for doing something which neither of them believes was wrong. When it comes to the point, he will probably find it easiest to pretend he has not noticed.

Few things are more damaging to religion than pretence. Clergy who have to pretend that they do not know what people are doing, people who have to pretend to their clergy that they are keeping the rules (for instance about contraception) when they are not, or pretend not to know that the minister knows what they are doing – all this breeds a kind of evasiveness, a tendency to be 'economical with the truth', which is all too quickly identified by outsiders as hypocrisy and creates an atmosphere of mistrust among Christians themselves. But what else can people do? We are told that four in ten marriages now end in divorce. Of these, many were solemnized in church, and some are of couples at least one of whom has remained a faithful church member. The parish priest, struggling to increase or at least maintain the size of the congregation, is in a dilemma. Is it worth risking turning one of these couples away because (if it keeps to its rules) the church can't welcome them? And, in any case, isn't the church supposed to be a community of sinners, and don't these people need its help and support at least as much as anyone else? Yet to bend the rules will immediately be called (at least by some) a 'concession' to the low moral standards of today. And what about young people sleeping together, or couples living together who are not married? Are they supposed to repent and mend their ways if they want to join the church? Of course Christians must speak out, as they always have, against prostitution, against the cheapening and commercialization of sex, against permissiveness of any kind. But what about couples (including homosexuals) who believe themselves fully committed to one another and with a good conscience give sexual expression to this commitment? What of young people who (as in many traditional cultures in the world) believe that sexual intercourse is one of the ways in which they must explore each other in order to build a relationship which (they genuinely hope) may result in lifelong commitment and marriage? These conventions (or 'patterns of intimacy') are now taken for granted by the majority of the population of most Western countries, with a corresponding rise in the divorce rate, in the commercial exploitation of sex and in one-parent families. Of course there is much in this to be deplored. The loosening of family ties and responsibilities encourages selfishness and undermines long-term commitment. A shallow and hedonistic view of sex is fostered and exploited by the media. There is an urgent job for Christians to do in promoting long-term, loving and self-sacrificing relationships in family life and resisting social pressures which are often merely permissive and sometimes even corrupting. If Christianity really is about love, then it is about real love and not about cheap and short-term relationships. It has genuine teaching to proclaim, and genuine standards which may be expected in the lives of those who profess it. The question is whether the church – any church – is helped to perform this task by having rules which either are not or cannot be observed by the majority of people in today's society or even by all its own members. Is it a good thing if Christians – particularly clergy – are forced to *pretend*?

It has to be said that the Church of England is in a particularly difficult position over all this. In the Roman Catholic Church the rules are clear (even if not always observed); but in the Church of England there is often doubt about what the rules really are. By the law of the land the clergy of the established church may marry any baptized person who is legally entitled to be married in a parish church. But according to the discipline of the church they should refuse to do so if that person has been divorced and has a spouse still living. If nevertheless they decide to solemnize that person's marriage they are within their legal rights. Until recently, this could of course be seen as ecclesiastical disobedience and could incur the displeasure of the bishop. But in the last twenty or thirty years even this discipline has been considerably relaxed. Many clergy feel that in certain deserving cases they can with a good conscience re-marry divorced persons; many bishops will give them permission to do so; and the church's General Synod has authorized certain procedures for putting this into effect. If it is really true that Jesus taught that marriage is 'indissoluble' (i.e. that the first marriage continues for ever and any subsequent marriage while the first partner is alive is sinful, if not actually bigamous) then the Church of England no longer faithfully witnesses to this teaching by the somewhat untidy rules it has adopted. Under certain circumstances these rules allow the clergy to marry persons who have been divorced and whose spouse is still living. So much for the 'doctrine' that marriage – any and every marriage – is indissoluble.

With regard to sex before or outside marriage the rules are even more obscure. Indeed it is difficult to know where to find them. As we shall see, the Bible is not by any means clear about it, and even if it were (as is apparently the case with homosexuality) it is at least arguable that the modern understanding of human nature, human sexuality and human social relationships makes it necessary for us to adapt its teaching to present day knowledge and conditions (as has indeed happened in the case of homosexuality). But where then shall we look for our 'rules'? Sexual behaviour (apart from adultery, which is forbidden in the Ten Commandments and has serious social consequences) has never been an item of Christian doctrine; and the Church of England has never had a body of canon law or official moral theology which would give authoritative guidance in such matters. All one can do is consult the writings of apparently respected church leaders and theologians. But there one will find, not rules, but a variety of opinions.

As always in the Church of England, the only way to test a matter of moral permissibility is to find an instance where there is some contact with the law. In this case it happens that an example is to hand. There are two ways in which it is possible to get married in the Church of England: either in a parish church after banns have been publicly called three times (to give an opportunity for anything irregular to be reported); or else by a Bishop's Licence, or (if the marriage is to be, say, in a college chapel) by a Special Licence from the Archbishop of Canterbury. The Archbishop's lawyers, who issue this Licence, have the job of doing what the calling of banns does, that is, making sure that there is nothing irregular. They will not issue it, for instance, if one of the parties has been divorced. But suppose the couple each put the same address on the form? The clear implication is that they are already cohabiting. If previous sexual relations were against the rules of the church, this would presumably count as an irregularity. The lawyers could hardly issue the Licence without at least asking a question about it. But not a word is said. Pretence again? Possibly. But hardly good evidence for the proposition that no sex before marriage is one of the rules of the church.

How important, in any case, are rules in the life of a church and its members? This is a difficult question, and is answered in different ways by different Christian traditions. Rules have always been prominent in the Roman Catholic Church, where they are formulated in an elaborate system of canon law and lay down the obligations, and also the rights, of every church member. Other churches are less rigorous; but all feel the need of certain rules in order to establish who is a member and who is not. No church could survive if it did not have some conditions of membership: someone who claimed to belong but who never came to a service or paid any subscription could hardly be taken seriously as a member. Just in order to maintain its identity and know who belongs a church needs to have rules. And since Christianity is a religion which makes high moral demands, members will be expected to live morally acceptable lives. Someone who indulges in blatantly un-Christian behaviour cannot expect to be welcome – though the church also claims to be a school for sinners and may be more interested in converting people from their evil ways and helping them to redeem their failures than in excluding them because they have broken the church's 'rules'. The main function of these rules is to define church membership. As in any society, if you keep them you have a right to be in; if you break them you risk being thrown out.

For historical reasons the Church of England is in an unusual position with regard to rules. There is a sense in which anyone living on the soil of England can claim to be a member; and though a list of 'duties of membership of the church' used to hang in the porches of many parish churches, these were never officially adopted and today there is no agreement about what the minimum obligations are. In the seventeenth century the Book of Common Prayer laid down one rule of membership: that one should attend communion three times a year. Today, most practising Christians would regard this as far too little; while some who never go at all would indignantly deny that this stops them from being members. After all, if they were baptized they have a legal right to be married in church, to attend any time they want to, and to have a funeral in church when they die. Who is to say they are not members?

The consequence is that the Church of England is a society with very blurred edges. If a vicar with the full support of the congregation makes a change in the form of Sunday worship, there may be violent protests from parishioners who seldom attend, are not on any church 'roll', but believe they have an absolute right to be listened to in such matters. They may be overruled because they are wrong or out of touch, but they cannot be ignored on the grounds that they are not 'members'. A bishop may make a public pronouncement which provokes violent disagreement in a letter to the press. The author of the letter may never be seen in church; but he will feel he has a perfect right to judge what a leader of 'his' church ought to say or do. For many, these blurred edges are frustrating. Church life might be much smoother if one knew exactly who was in and who was out and who was entitled to make a fuss if something is changed. A few more rules, on this view, would be a positive advantage. But others see the advantage the other way. The reason why the Church of England continues to have a far greater influence than its numbers seem to warrant is precisely because so many people have a basic loyalty to it even if they are not practising Christians. To make more rules would be to shut them out permanently. And should not the church, of all societies, have an ever-open door?

Given this history of unwillingness in the Church of England to impose rules on its members, it is all the more surprising that it has particularly strict rules about divorce and remarriage. As recently as 1957 the discipline of the Church of England was authoritatively stated as follows: 'The Church should not allow the use of the Marriage Service in the case of anyone who has a former partner still living' – based on the dogmatic statement that 'marriage after divorce during the lifetime of a former partner always involves a departure from the true principle of marriage as declared by Our Lord'.[1] Notice that nothing is said about divorce itself. This is nowhere explicitly forbidden – how could it be? Divorces take place every day, and often involve church members. There is nothing the church can do to 'forbid' them, though it may do everything in its power to discourage them. Moreover (as we shall see) there is only one Gospel text which specifically bans divorce apart from

[1] *Act of Convocation*, 1957

remarriage, and St Paul himself seems to allow for it under certain circumstances. What is being outlawed here is *remarriage* after divorce. Even this is permissible, apparently, if the first (divorced) partner has died, so divorce *in itself* cannot constitute a bar, either to church membership or to remarriage. What is forbidden is remarriage while the first partner is alive. The grounds for this are said to lie in the teaching of Jesus, who (it is widely believed) taught that a marriage is 'indissoluble'. It follows that it is not divorce which causes the problem, but the nature of marriage itself. If marriage – any marriage – is indeed indissoluble, this means that it creates a relationship that nothing (except death) can alter – rather like the relationship between brother and sister. It makes no difference if the first marriage was entirely unsuccessful and 'died'. It makes no difference if the second marriage is perfectly happy and appears to be abundantly 'blessed'. If the first partner is still alive the couple remain on awkward terms with the church. They cannot have their marriage solemnized, and for many years they may be denied full rights of membership (they may be forbidden, for instance, to receive communion). It makes no difference if they believe in their hearts that this second marriage was 'right', and if they present to the world outside a model of married and family life that appears profoundly 'Christian'. In the eyes of the church they are permanently compromised. They are public sinners, in that they have failed to uphold the church's standard of lifelong union; they are (technically) unrepentant, in that they refuse to return to their original spouse; and their second marriage is somehow tinged with bigamy owing to the alleged continued existence of the first.

In other words, not merely is this rule uncharacteristic of the church's usual approach to sin and failure (which is that you can always make a new start) but it is a rule that applies specifically to just one part of the problem. It does not forbid divorce; if there is a divorce and the first partner dies, it does not forbid remarriage; if someone remarries after divorce, and *then* the former spouse dies, he or she suddenly becomes entirely respectable again in the eyes of the church. The one thing that is forbidden is remarriage *while the first partner is alive*. The only possible reason for this rule is that the first marriage continues in some sense to exist unless one of the spouses dies. It is 'indissoluble' – except by death.

I have said that the existence of such a rule is in any case uncharacteristic of the Church of England, which has never had much enthusiasm for drawing lines between those who are and are not (or cannot be) members. What *is* characteristic is the way in which this rule is observed (or not observed) in practice. The Archbishop of Canterbury's guidance to the clergy of his diocese contains a tell-tale phrase: 'It is not the normal practice of the Church of England to marry where a former partner is still alive.' Not *normal*? Does this mean there is an 'abnormal' practice? Is the rule sometimes broken? Indeed it is. In 1981 a vote in the General Synod showed a majority in favour of second marriages being allowed. Since then, many bishops have instructed their clergy that, if certain conditions were fulfilled, they would give permission; and many faithful church people have now had their second marriages performed in church and are fully accepted as members. But what seems not to have been noticed is that the only justification for the rule in the first place was that Jesus had taught that marriage is 'indissoluble'. If this is true, there can be no exceptions. One cannot make some marriages 'soluble' just by deciding that, in certain cases, a second marriage may be authorized. If the doctrine is true, the first marriage still exists and a second marriage, even if not bigamous in the eyes of the law, is certainly sinful and ought not to be entered upon. If the doctrine is not true, then there was no ground for the rule in the first place (other than one saying of Jesus which appears to be contradicted by others). But today the church both continues to proclaim the rule in theory while in practice it admits exceptions. Pretence again?

In the next chapter we must consider whether Jesus ever intended us to have such a rule in the first place. But first let us look briefly at another area where pretence seems more common than honesty, that of sexual relationships before marriage. I say 'before marriage' rather than 'outside marriage', because if one of the parties is married the act involves adultery, and about this there need be little argument. Adultery is firmly forbidden in the Bible, and for good reason. It makes no difference if one calls it 'an affair': if one, or both, of those involved are married, the consequences are liable to be destructive of their marriage, harmful for the children and damaging for society. But sex *before* marriage is a different matter. So is sex between homosexuals. What are the rules about this?

There are traditional ways of describing these acts. The first is 'fornication', the second is 'sodomy'. In the Bible, fornication is always a sin, and Sodom is a by-word for wickedness. So it seems the church has no choice. Fornication and sodomy are sinful by definition, and must be condemned. Indeed, in the Book of Common

Prayer it is stated that marriage was 'ordained for a remedy against sin, and to avoid fornication'. This seems to settle the matter. The dictionary defines fornication as intercourse with someone who is unmarried, or married to someone else, and sodomy as intercourse between males. The words cover all sexual acts before or outside marriage and those between men (and, by implication, between women). But they also denote sins. It follows that all acts of this kind are sinful.

But to argue like this is like arguing that any act of homicide ought to attract the heaviest penalty because killing is murder and murder is the most serious of crimes. The question that has to be asked is, Is all killing necessarily murder? Plainly it is not: it may be in self-defence, or carried out by a soldier under orders in time of war. Similarly with fornication. We can agree that it is always sinful. But we still have to ask whether it covers *all* intercourse outside marriage. And on this question, as on that of homosexual inter-course, it is much more difficult to give a clear answer. There is doubt about the meaning of the Greek word *porneia*, which is the word in the New Testament traditionally translated 'fornication'. There is doubt about what the 'sin of Sodom' really was and whether the harsh things said about it in the New Testament apply to all homosexual behaviour. There is the influence of St Augustine to be taken into account, who held all sexual intercourse to be sinful – even in marriage, unless it was strictly necessary for the procreation of children. Neither the Bible nor church history give an altogether clear answer on exactly what does and does not constitute 'fornica-tion'. Certain things, of course, are consistently condemned: adultery, prostitution, bestiality, incest. None of these has ever been controversial. But on the question, for example, of sexual relations between two adults who live together, have formed a long-term and committed relationship and intend to get married some time in the future it is far from obvious what the church's 'rule' could be based on. Yet it is this presumed rule which makes so many clergy feel they must pretend not to have noticed when faced by a couple who are co-habiting while preparing for their marriage.

It is often said that in recent years moral standards have declined and that the church has done too little to recall people to the stricter rules of the past. Both parts of this judgment are questionable. In some respects one could argue that moral principles are at least as strong as they ever were. Offences against human rights evoke immediate protest. The victims of disaster receive generous aid from the public. Blood donors continue to offer blood for no reward other than knowing that they are helping others. In sexual matters, of course, things have changed. Marriage is no longer the only recognized form of family life; homosexual relationships have been legalized and socially accepted; young people regularly sleep together long before they are married. There are also tendencies of a distinctly evil kind. The commercial exploitation of sex is abhorrent to most people, and sexual abuse of children has become so prevalent that the government has been forced to tighten legislation. The church should certainly have much to say about all this. It should certainly continue its fight against all forms of prostitution, victimization, abuse and the other evils which attend sexual permissiveness. But it does not follow that it should have a negative view of all the changes that have taken place. If its own rules are not clear, it must not be pushed into uttering a blanket condemnation of every change in traditional moral standards. Some of these changes may actually be for the good.

I began by saying that Christianity is about love, and should have something helpful to say about marriage, family and sexual relationships. This I firmly believe. The promises which people make when they get married are of profound significance and are enriched and strengthened by the central beliefs of the Christian faith. 'Promise' is therefore a key theme of this book. But before getting on to it we must ask whether the church has rightly interpreted what scripture has to say on those matters, and whether it has relied on a correct understanding of human nature in formulating its doctrine of marriage. Are its rules such as to promote a lasting relationship of love and mutual commitment, or do they involve both ministers and people in a damaging pantomime of compromise and pretence?

2

No Divorce?

What did Jesus have to say about all this?

Most people would assume that the first place to look for an answer is in the Gospels. And certainly there are passages in all four Gospels where Jesus is reported to have said something relevant to our subject. But nowadays scholars may warn us that this is not the best place to begin. The letters of St Paul (those, at least, which he certainly wrote or dictated) were written before about AD 60. The earliest of the Gospels (probably Mark) is unlikely to have been completed until some years later. Of course it may contain material which dates back to a period earlier than Paul's letters; but we cannot always be certain of this, whereas what we can be certain of is that Paul had things to say about marriage and divorce, some of which he believed to go back to Jesus himself. So that is where we should start.

As a matter of fact, Paul makes it particularly easy for us to discover what Jesus said (or what he believed Jesus said) by telling us exactly when he is quoting Jesus and when he is not. He devotes several paragraphs of his First Letter to the Corinthians to these questions. Not that he was in the business of writing treatises on such subjects. His letters were not intended to give comprehensive teaching on Christian faith and morals, but to deal with particular questions that had cropped up in the life of the young churches for which he felt responsible. At the beginning of I Corinthians 7, Paul appears to quote an actual sentence from a letter he had received from the Corinthians: 'It is good if a man does not touch a woman.' This suggests that some at least of the Christians in Corinth had taken the line that Christianity was an ascetic religion and that a Christian should forswear all sexual intercourse (which is what 'touching a woman' almost certainly means in this context). Paul agrees with this in so far as he will make no concession to 'fornication'; but he absolutely disagrees with it so far as marriage is concerned, and his first comment lays down the principles of the relationship between wife and husband, and the 'rights' of each over their bodies, in a way that can hardly be faulted even by the most egalitarian standards of today (7.3–5). After this he goes on to commend celibacy to those who are unmarried or who are widows, partly on the grounds of his own experience (we do not know if he had ever been married or not, but he was certainly single when he wrote), partly on the principle that 'it is better to marry than to burn', words that have done no small harm to his reputation in modern times (though they may in fact have a more subtle meaning which makes them less offensive).[1] And then he reaches the point that interests us:

> To the married I give this ruling, which is not mine but the Lord's: a wife must not separate herself from her husband – if she does, she must either remain unmarried or be reconciled to her husband – and the husband must not divorce his wife (7.10–11).

Here, then, we have a definite ruling against divorce; and this (Paul obligingly tells us) is on the authority of 'the Lord', that is, Jesus. This, as we shall see, would have been enough to distinguish Christians from their neighbours. Both in Jewish and in pagan society divorce was relatively frequent and was regulated by law. But Christians were to be different: among them, no divorce!

But if we are tempted to think that this settles anything for Christians or the church today, we need to look at the passage more closely. It tells us, certainly, that Jesus was against divorce. This is not in itself surprising, and no one has ever seriously doubted it. Our question is whether he made an absolute *rule* against divorce; and on this the text gives an answer no clearer than the other passages we shall be considering later. Indeed it seems to point in the opposite direction. No divorce for Christians – that is the grand principle that Paul attributes to Jesus. Then he goes on, 'But if someone does . . .' In other words Paul allowed for exceptions. It may have been a principle: he repeats it at the end of the chapter ('A wife is bound to her husband as long as he lives' 7.39). But it was a principle that allowed of exceptions. And in the very next paragraph he gives an instance of what such an exception might be, and tells us that this is

---

[1] 'To burn' may mean, not to burn with unsatisfied sexual desire, but to be tested by God's purifying judgment

his own, not Jesus', judgment. In the case of a couple in which one of the spouses is an unbeliever, it is good if they remain together if they can without dissension; otherwise they should part (7.15). In other words, divorce should be avoided as far as possible. But there might be occasions for it: it was not an absolute rule.

But what about the situation *after* divorce? On this Paul seems to give a ruling:

> ' . . . if she does (divorce) she must either remain unmarried or be reconciled to her husband' (7.11)

Yet once again there are problems. Paul does not tell us whether he is still quoting Jesus or whether this is a ruling he has added on his own authority. If the latter, we can think of reasons why he may have said it. We know from a number of remarks in his letters that at this stage he encouraged an attitude in the church such as is found from time to time in enthusiastic religious movements: the present time is a crisis of enormous significance, at any moment something may happen – you could call it 'the end of the world' – which will radically affect the condition of everyone's life, and the essential thing is to be ready, alert and as little encumbered as possible. For this reason Paul advised Christians not to get involved in marriage if they could help it. If (as is likely) he is not quoting Jesus with regard to remarriage, his apparent ruling against it may simply be another application of his own general principle that the emergency is so great that it is better to be without domestic entanglements.

All this may sound rather negative, as if Paul regarded marriage as something of a nuisance to be put up with rather than as a source of blessing and fulfilment. And this may be true, at least when Paul was in the mood to concentrate on the signs of the times and encourage people to prepare for a new age. But even the most enthusiastic visionaries seldom keep this up all the time; and later on we shall see that Paul (or possibly one of his followers) also took a much more positive view of marriage and wrote a paragraph which has been a source of inspiration for married life down the centuries. For the present, we can sum up what Paul (our earliest source) tells us as follows:

- Jesus was against divorce.
- Christians might nevertheless occasionally divorce (or at least separate).

- If they did, they should not remarry – either because Jesus was also against remarriage, or because Paul was against any marriage that was not necessary, or both.

In other words, we can tell from Paul what sort of marriage discipline he thought should be observed in the church, and he supported this with a clear principle derived from Jesus: no divorce. What we can *not* discover is whether he thought that marriage is 'indissoluble' (which seems unlikely, given the exceptions he allowed for from the general rule), nor whether Jesus ruled out marriage after a divorce. For this we shall have to turn to the slightly later evidence of the Gospels.

Of course, this evidence may not be later at all. The fact that the Gospels were written some years after Paul's lifetime does not mean that sayings of Jesus which they preserve may not be much older – indeed, may not represent (though in another language from that which Jesus probably spoke) the words which he actually said. Nevertheless Paul stands closer to the source and origin of the traditions about Jesus than any Gospel writer, and it is important to notice what he, at that early stage, believed Jesus had said and what standards of marriage and divorce in the church he thought best reflected the Lord's teaching. We may be able to use this as some sort of control if we find that there are difficulties in interpreting the relevant texts in the Gospels.

So, still following our assumed chronological sequence, we may start by looking at Mark's Gospel. This contains just one passage which deals with our subject, and it may be helpful to set this out in full.

He was asked: 'Is it lawful for a man to divorce his wife?' This question was put to test him. He responded by asking, 'What did Moses command you?' They answered, 'Moses permitted a man to divorce his wife by a certificate of dismissal.' Jesus said to them, 'It was because of your stubbornness that he made this rule for you. But in the beginning, at the creation, "God made them male and female. That is why a man leaves his father and mother, and is united to his wife, and the two become one flesh." It follows that they are no longer two individuals: they are one flesh. Therefore what God has joined together, man must not separate' (Mark 10.2–8).

Like the passage in St Paul, this leaves us in no doubt that Jesus was against divorce. And before going any further it may be helpful to ask whether this set him apart from his contemporaries in the same way as a church which tried to forbid divorce would have been set apart from the society around it. What did other people think about it? Was it generally permitted or generally approved of? Were there others who took the same view as Jesus?

These questions are not difficult to answer. Jewish society, like the pagan societies surrounding it, recognized divorce. It also recognized polygamy, though it is unlikely that this was often taken advantage of. No law was necessary to legalize these things. What was required was legal protection for a wife who was for one reason or another discarded by her husband. In law, the most important right for a divorced wife was freedom to marry again. The wife was, in effect, the husband's property until he formally renounced his claim to her. The law therefore compelled him to give her a 'certificate of divorce' which made her free to marry again. But the law also imposed a financial penalty on a husband who divorced his wife for anything less serious than adultery: he had to repay a sum of money. To this extent the law could be said to have discouraged divorce.

All this was based on a single clause of the Law of Moses (Deut. 24.1–4), a passage which is not primarily about divorce at all, but about remarrying one's former wife (it was probably a law originally passed to control wife-swopping!). The clause assumes that if a man divorces his wife it is because he has 'found something offensive in her'; it also assumes that he will give her a certificate of divorce. This text (which is one of those quoted in the discussion between Jesus and the Pharisees) spawned a prodigious amount of legal opinion. Exactly what constituted 'something offensive', and exactly what circumstances entitled a divorced wife to claim financial compensation, were matters on which there was lively debate. What a court would decide in any particular case will have depended on the view taken by individual judges, and may have been difficult to predict. But in general we may say that the law had an interest in restricting easy divorce, and it could do so by tightening the rules implied by the text in Deuteronomy.

However, it was not only lawyers who were concerned about divorce. The fact that something is legal does not mean that it is always desirable. There can always be a moral standard that is considerably higher than the minimum imposed by law. This was certainly the case here. Moral teachers took their cue from the prophet Malachi:

'Let none of you be unfaithful to the wife of your youth' (2.15).

What the prophet was inveighing against was probably an abuse prevalent in his own time: discarding an ageing wife in order to have more children by a younger one. But the prophet used solemn words which applied to any divorce:

'You have broken faith with her, though she is your partner, your wife by solemn covenant' (2.14).

And subsequent teachers stressed the moral obligation which any husband has to his wife – 'Let the wife of your youth be blessed; find your joy in her' (Prov. 5.18) – and the inestimable value of a good wife, who is a 'gift from the Lord' (Prov. 19.14). To strengthen this view of the marriage bond such teachers sometimes turned to Genesis, with its account of the creation of human beings as 'male and female', and of the way a man 'leaves his father and mother and attaches himself to his wife and the two become one' (Gen. 1.27; 2.24). These texts – which also occur in Jesus' discussion – could be used to promote a genuine partnership in marriage, as in this verse from Tobit in the Apocrypha:

'You made Adam and also Eve his wife who was to be his partner and support' (8.6).

In short, the Jewish moral tradition not only tried to discourage divorce, but it promoted what we might call a high view of marriage: not just a means of acquiring wealth and having children but a lifelong partnership of love and mutual support. Yet at the same time these teachers were realistic (at least from the husband's point of view!). 'There is nothing so bad as a bad wife!' (Ecclus. 25.19). Her nagging can become like 'the continual dripping of rain' (Prov. 19.13). It can reach a point where the only sensible thing to do is to 'bring the marriage to an end' (Ecclus. 25.26).

We are told in two of the Gospel accounts that a question about divorce was put to Jesus 'tempting' or 'testing' him. How we understand this depends on whether we think Jesus was answering as a lawyer or as a moral and religious teacher. If as a lawyer, the test will have been whether he could give an interpretation of existing statutes that would support his own view; if as a moralist, it will have been a question whether he was proposing a standard so different from that of normal society that he need hardly be taken seriously by practical lawyers. As we shall see, Matthew's Gospel reports the discussion as if it was indeed between lawyers. But Mark's version, with which we have begun, requires some study before we can be sure. It ends with a statement which has all the marks of a legal judgment:

> 'Whoever divorces his wife and remarries commits adultery against her; so too if she divorces her husband and remarries, she commits adultery' (10.11–12).

As it stands, it is often thought that this could not be a Jewish legal judgment, since technically in Jewish law a wife could not institute divorce proceedings (though she may have had other ways of bringing about a divorce); Jesus' original words may have been adapted to the situation under Roman law, where divorce was equally available to the wife. But this does not affect the point that the sentence has a distinctively legal *form*. 'Whoever does x receives the consequence y.' This is how countless laws are formulated. Does this mean that Jesus must have been legislating?

This is a key question, and the answer to it will have great importance for everything we want to say about the Christian approach to marriage and divorce. If Jesus was giving a legal judgment, then it would follow that he had placed his authority behind a new law which his church would then be bound to observe, and which would appear to allow for no exceptions. If on the other hand he was speaking as a moral teacher, we should regard his teaching as setting a high moral standard but not as imposing a rule that could never be broken. Which of these is the correct view?

To answer this, we need first to make up our minds whether law-giving and law-making was something in which Jesus was ever involved. Unlike ourselves, who are used to a parliament continually making new laws, the people among whom Jesus lived had a statute book that could neither be changed nor added to because it was believed to have been given to them many centuries before by God. This was the law which governed every case that came before the courts. The task of the judges was to determine the application of this ancient law-book to the circumstances of their day and to agree on the appropriate judgment, verdict and sentence. With regard to divorce cases, as we have seen, they would have had no power to prevent the divorce taking place; their responsibility was to protect the rights of the wife and decide whether the husband should pay compensation to her. On these questions, different schools of lawyers (of which the Pharisees were one) might take different views. The outcome of the case would often depend on the composition of the court.

If, then, Jesus was making a legal judgment, we have to ask where he would have fitted into this system. It is often suggested that he was making new laws, or superseding the Law of Moses. In the matter of divorce, this would presumably have meant declaring that the implied permission to divorce which was found in Deuteronomy was not valid, and that anyone found proceeding with a divorce could be prosecuted for a criminal offence like adultery which (theoretically at least) carried the death penalty. Quite apart from the question whether Jesus would seriously have intended couples who divorced to be stoned to death, we have to ask how such a change in the law could have been put into effect. How could judges, who already disagreed on the subject, have been persuaded that they must now follow a quite different ruling? How would lawyers, who regarded the Law of Moses as by definition unalterable, be led to accept that this teacher from Nazareth had authority to change the very ground-rules of their profession? And even if they were, would they not have observed that polygamy was still legal, so that anyone who wished (and could afford) to separate from his first wife and marry a second would be free to do so? The practical difficulties in the way of any such reform would have been so daunting that it seems highly unlikely that this was what Jesus intended.

But this is not necessarily what is meant by a 'new law'. Might not Jesus have been legislating, not for society in general, but for his own followers? We have an example of this in the Dead Sea Scrolls, where the community had its own rules about marriage and definitely forbade polygamy – and it is significant that they based their argument for doing so on the verse from Genesis ('male and female created he them', 1.27) which was also quoted by Jesus. Any religious movement or sect is likely to have its own rules of conduct, and if these were laid down by the founder it makes sense to say that he was 'making a new law'. Jesus certainly started a movement, and much of his teaching takes the form of instructions on how they should behave. May we not say that in this instance, at least, he was telling them that they should not refer to the existing Law of Moses, but should be governed by a new and stricter law imposed by himself?

This makes good sense – but only if this is what Jesus was doing the rest of the time. Did his teaching normally take the form of rules to be observed by his followers? Indeed, was it his intention to found a community that would be bound by a strict discipline? Again, we have an example of such a community in the Dead Sea Scrolls, and there existed other sects in his time which lived under particular rules of their own that were more demanding than the law of the land. But there is one feature of any such community which must be noticed. To be a member of it, one had to keep the rules. If one did not keep them there would be penalties; if one refused to conform one would be thrown out. It is true that since very early times such sects have existed within Christianity – churches or societies which have claimed to take their inspiration from the Gospels and have made strict rules for their members, not just on sexual conduct, but on such things as military service, consuming alcohol, smoking, swearing and working on Sundays. All of these have been ready to exclude people who did not conform. But the great majority of readers of the Gospels, and all the mainstream churches, have interpreted Jesus' teaching in a more open way. Did not Jesus call, not the righteous, but sinners to repentance? Did he not deliberately consort with people whose moral conduct fell below the standards set by the respectable society of his day? Did he not actually say that tax-collectors and prostitutes would qualify for entry to the Kingdom of Heaven before the religious leaders of his own people? (Matt. 21.31). It is difficult to imagine such a teacher laying down rules which would have excluded many of his hearers from following him (for divorce was by no means uncommon). And in fact most churches have felt that they were being most faithful to his teaching when they welcomed sinners of any kind and worked for their repentance rather than excluding some on principle because they had broken a particular rule.

It looks, then, as if a strict rule on divorce would have been uncharacteristic of Jesus. Of course his teaching is often demanding to a very high degree. The Sermon on the Mount is proverbial for setting standards that few people feel able to measure up to. When giving his moral teaching Jesus had a distinctive style. He loved a touch of exaggeration – a camel going through the eye of a needle, a plank in your own eye compared with a speck of dust in someone else's. He startled people by taking an extreme case; not just ordinary family duties, but the normally over-riding one of seeing to the burial of one's father, must take second place to following Jesus (Matt. 8.21–22). At times he resorted almost to paradox – turn the other cheek, go the second mile. All this was well in the tradition of moral teaching. There was no suggeston that there ought to be new laws to force people into such conduct. How could there be? Nor could Jesus possibly have imagined that he was founding a community in which these radical demands became rules for membership. Jesus was making use of the traditional repertory of a moral teacher, but giving old maxims a twist that would jolt people out of their complacency and open their eyes to new dangers and new possibilities in their moral conduct.

And yet, as we noticed, the saying about divorce has a legal form. 'Whoever divorces and remarries commits adultery.' This is exactly how countless laws are phrased, both in the Hebrew scriptures and in other law codes: whoever does x must expect the consequence y. Does this mean that, whatever may be true of Jesus' teaching on other subjects, on this one matter he intended to create an absolute rule? Before coming to this conclusion we need to take two points into account. First, our saying is *not* exactly like a legal formula. Consider the following from Hebrew law:

If anyone strikes his victim with anything made of iron, and he dies, then he is a murderer; the murderer must be put to death (Num. 35.16).

Hebrew law, that is to say, does not merely define what is illegal; it also prescribes the sentence. So with adultery:

If a man commits adultery with another man's wife . . . both adulterer and adulteress must be put to death (Lev. 20.10).

Compared with this, Jesus' saying is incomplete: it lacks the penalty. If it is to be exactly comparable it needs to be completed:

'Whoever divorces and remarries commits adultery, and must be put to death' (or excluded from the community, or whatever penalty Jesus might have had in mind).

As it stands, it is hardly law. But there is also a second point. I referred a moment ago to Jesus using the repertory of a moral teacher. The standard items in this repertory were maxims ('A wise

son makes a glad father') and commands ('Listen to your father who
begot you').[2] The object was to persuade people to behave better,
and the means chosen were, as always, the carrot or the stick: It is
sensible to do this rather than that; or, Do this, or else . . . But
occasionally a moralist might make his point in a sharper way by
adopting the style of a law-giver. There is a good example in an
ancient Jewish saying:

> He that talks much with womankind brings evil upon himself and
> neglects the study of the law and at the last will inherit Gehenna.[3]

The form is exactly the legal one we have been looking at: whoever
does x will incur the penalty y. But the moment we have taken in
what it is saying we realize that it has got nothing to do with law. No
human court could ever take seriously the charge of talking too much
(whether or not to a woman!); and no human judge could ever
sentence a criminal to hell-fire. The speaker is a moralist, not a
lawyer. He is not proposing an addition to any existing code of laws.
He is simply drawing attention to the serious consequences of
wasting time (I am afraid this is how he saw it!) with women. And to
do so he uses a form which has the solemn and rather threatening
sound of a page from the statute book.

This example takes us close to some sayings that are attributed to
Jesus. One in particular is very similar:

> Whoever is angry with his brother shall be liable to judgment . . .
> and whoever shall say, 'You fool', shall be liable to the fire of
> Gehenna (Matt. 5.22).

Once again the form is legal: whoever does x is liable to y. And the
word 'judgment' reinforces the impression that we have to do with a
matter of law. But of course the impression is illusory. No court
would take seriously a charge that someone had merely been angry;
and no human judge can send a man to hell. Once we have taken this
in we realize that Jesus is certainly not speaking as a lawyer. He is
using a legal form to draw attention to the seriousness of something
which most people might regard as trivial. One would not normally
think that there was much wrong in being angry from time to time.
But occasionally it can do great damage. By using a formula

[2] Prov. 10.1; 23.22
[3] Mishnah, *Aboth* 1.5

appropriate to a serious legal offence, Jesus alerts us to possible consequences which we might otherwise not think of. There are occasions on which anger is a very grave fault indeed. Lest we should forget it, Jesus startles us by making us wonder if it ought to be somehow totally avoided.

It is significant that this saying on anger occurs in a series of three pronouncements of Jesus all of which have the same form: whoever does x will incur the consequence y. These are all in the Sermon on the Mount (Matt. 5.21–32). The next in the series is again pseudo-legal.

> Anyone who looks at a woman with a lustful eye has already committed adultery with her in his heart.

The addition of the words, 'in his heart', makes it plain that this is a saying about intentions and possible consequences, not about acts that may be criminal or forbidden. But even without them it would need only a little thought to realize that, though the form is legal, it is inconceivable that court proceedings should be the result of a flirtatious glance. The speaker is giving moral teaching, not pro-posing reform of the legal code. But this saying shows a striking similarity with the third and last in the series, which is the one from which we started. In its form in Matthew it runs:

> Anyone who divorces his wife, save in a matter of unchastity, causes her to be involved in adultery, and whoever marries her commits adultery.

The difference, of course, is that a moment's reflection shows that whereas neither of the other two could have been meant to be a law or a rule, this *could* be one. It is perfectly possible to imagine a court regarding any marriage to a divorced person as adultery, or a community imposing a strict rule against divorce and remarriage. Both of these have actually been the case in the history of the church.

Other forms of this saying occur elsewhere. But in this one there is a tell-tale phrase:

> . . . save in a matter of unchastity . . .

This makes an exception to the general rule: divorce and remarriage is equivalent to adultery *except* when there has been sexual misconduct. But you cannot have an exception unless there is a rule; and this shows that the author of this Gospel did take it to be a rule.

Perhaps the community to which he was writing already lived by this rule. Certainly we saw that Paul believed Jesus had given a rule, though he too allowed for exceptions. But Mark and Luke say nothing about unchastity or about any exception. We cannot be sure that Matthew and Paul got it right. If Jesus did not mean this to be a rule, what did he mean?

Let us go back for a moment to the two previous sayings. Jesus was talking about bursts of anger and flirtatious glances, things that we should not normally regard as very serious. But of course they *can* be serious; and, to alert us to this, Jesus, the moral teacher, describes them as very serious indeed – in one case as incurring an eternal punishment (Gehenna), in the other as being equivalent to the capital crime of adultery. It was his characteristic way of pressing a point home by exaggerating, making consequences which we would not normally worry about seem so serious that we have to rethink our whole attitude. Now divorce, in his time, was rather similar. It was relatively frequent, and often obtained for quite trivial reasons. Would it not have been along the grain of Jesus' teaching to say the same kind of thing about this as about anger and flirting? Other moral teachers, as we have seen, took a stronger line on divorce than the lawyers did. It would have been characteristic of Jesus to take a stronger line still: divorce is as bad as adultery – which means (since adultery could be punished by death), very bad indeed!

There is a case therefore for saying that this saying of Jesus on divorce, at least in the form preserved in Mark (which is probably the earliest version) was originally, not a law or a rule, but a moral injunction, fully in Jesus' characteristic style and causing some amazement among his contemporaries who took divorce for granted: divorce is equivalent to adultery!

Now of course it could be said that I have skewed the whole question by concentrating on divorce rather than remarriage. What Jesus actually said was, 'Whoever divorces his wife *and marries another* is committing adultery.'[4] May not Jesus be permitting divorce after all, and merely condemning remarriage *after* divorce? It is here that we need to go back to St Paul. As we saw, he certainly believed that Jesus was against divorce. If he knew the saying we are concerned with, he must have understood it to refer to divorce as much as remarriage – and who are we, two thousand years later, to

---

[4] Luke 16.18. This is the simplest, and possibly most authentic, form of the saying

think we know better? If he did not know this saying, then he must have known one like it which made it clear that Jesus' target was the prevalence of divorce. Moreover, the distinction is somewhat unreal. Then, as now, the great majority of men who divorced did so in order to remarry, and the point of the 'certificate' which the husband had to give to his ex-wife was that it enabled *her* to re-marry. Divorce and remarriage went together: Jesus could hardly have targeted one without the other. And by adding remarriage to divorce he was able to sharpen his point. Divorce is not just *as bad* as adultery: if it is followed by remarriage it is also *like* adultery because it involves a relationship with another woman or man. And adultery was a capital crime, the subject of one of the Ten Commandments.

But the proof that Jesus was concerned with divorce and not just with remarriage is in the main part of his discussion with the Pharisees which we quoted at the outset. This passage also has been invoked to show that Jesus intended to lay down an absolute rule, and this time there is no doubt that it is divorce he is talking about. The question put to him is quite specific: 'Is it lawful for a man to divorce his wife?' The answer, of course, could be read off from the existing law. This, as we have seen, was concerned with the protection of a divorced wife (or of a husband whose wife was unfaithful). It did not have to 'permit' divorce: it laid down the conditions under which a divorce could be obtained. So the legal answer was clear; divorce is permitted. But Jesus then went on to quote two sentences from the creation story in Genesis:

'God made them male and female' (1.27)
' . . . the two become one flesh' (2.24)

These texts were never (so far as we know) quoted by lawyers in connection with divorce; but they were used by moral teachers who were trying to strengthen marriage and discourage divorce. This is a first indication that, here too, Jesus was not formulating a law or a rule but was speaking of a moral imperative.

What use did he make of these texts? For our purpose (and apparently for his) the most significant of them was the phrase, 'the two become one flesh'. This is a very paradoxical statement. In any literal or practical sense it is plainly untrue: man and wife are two individuals, not one. At the very least we have to say, *it is as if* they become one flesh. In what respect do they do this? Because of the word 'flesh', it is almost inevitable that we should think of their sexual relationship (which is how St Paul takes it in another context, as we shall see). But this is not the only possibility. They could be 'one' equally in terms of domestic partnership, mutual love or the sharing of house and family. One Jewish rabbi understood it in terms of kinship – a man's wife is 'one flesh' with him in the same way as other members of his family are, and remains so even after a divorce.[5] Certainly it implies that they are bound together in an intimate union. But, so far as we know, none of Jesus' Jewish contemporaries inferred from this that divorce was impossible or even in every case undesirable. At most it strengthened the notion of commitment or 'covenant' between husband and wife. To support his more radical approach, Jesus needed something stronger than this.

In fact, he proceeded to draw an inference from it which he expressed in a somewhat oracular form – oracular, because (like any oracle) it does not make clear exactly what is needed for it to be fulfilled. 'What God has joined together let no man put asunder.' How are we to know what God has 'joined together'? Is God responsible for any and every marriage? This is certainly not implied by the passage in Genesis; indeed, it is the man, not God, who takes the initiative when he 'leaves father and mother and is united to his wife'. In all legal and religious marriage ceremonies the man and the woman take full responsibility for what they are doing: 'Forasmuch as N and N have consented in holy wedlock . . . ' Jesus cannot have meant that things are taken out of their hands and arranged entirely by God. There was, it is true, a Jewish belief that 'marriages are made in heaven', that is, intended by God – just as we may say today, 'They were meant for each other'. But this did not mean that divorce was impossible. Even if it did, no one would have thought that *all* marriages were made in heaven; and how was one to be certain which ones were? – which perhaps gives us a clue to Jesus' meaning. It would have been absolutely characteristic of him to have taken the *possibility* that a marriage was 'made in heaven' as the basis for a radical position about divorce. Of any given marriage it *might* be the case that God had ordained it. In case that was so – in case this was one that God had 'joined together' – no one should take the risk of flying against God's will by having a divorce. 'What God has joined together let no man put asunder' then becomes a solemn warning:

---

[5] Midrash Genesis Rabbah 17.3

never contemplate divorce, for you might be breaking up something that God has put together.

We have now looked at all the teaching of Jesus that bears directly on marriage and divorce, and I have suggested a way in which it may be understood and interpreted. Of course there is much more that could be said. Innumerable scholarly discussions of these texts have been written, and there is no single agreed interpretation. I certainly would not wish to claim that my own must be right. What I have been doing is in fact much more modest. I have been looking at the texts to see if they enable us to answer the question, Did Jesus intend to lay down an absolute rule about divorce, or was he doing what he did with regard to every other moral issue he addressed? Was he legislating or was he challenging us to look at marriage in a new way and to realize the seriousness of doing anything less than a loving God desires us to do? My conclusion is that Jesus was neither attempting to get a new law on to the statute book nor laying down an absolute rule for his followers, but was using his characteristic style of exaggeration and paradox, taking the extreme case and startling his hearers with a radical proposal: no divorce under any circumstances! That his teaching was indeed startling is conveyed by his disciples' reaction. In that case, they said, might it be better not to marry at all? (Matt. 19.10). No one doubts that he set a higher standard for marriage than any of his contemporaries would have thought possible. But that does not mean that he was laying down a rule such that, if any of his followers failed to keep it, they would be unable to do what Jesus invited them to do in every other aspect of their moral life: repent and be forgiven.

Again, I cannot claim to have proved my point. Other views will continue to be held for as long as scholars continue to study the texts. When a view similar to mine was presented in a Church of England Report on marriage, another commission a few years later reported the criticism that it was 'suspiciously close to the main recommendation of the Report as a whole'.[6] Doubtless the same could be said of my own research: I have succeeded in reaching the conclusion I wanted! But for my purposes it is not necessary to demonstrate that this is what Jesus must have meant. All that is required is to be able to say that it is *possible* to take his teaching as an example of strong moral pressure rather than of law-giving or rule-making. And this I

[6] *Marriage and the Church's Task*, 1978, p. 136

believe can be argued, and has a wide range of support in the scholarly world. It follows that any church which claims to have a law or absolute rule about divorce and remarriage, and that this is based on scripture, has built its doctrine on a shaky foundation.

But this, of course, is not the only reason why churches have made rules against remarriage after divorce. We must now look at some of the other arguments which have been used.

3

No Remarriage?

Jesus was against divorce. That statement is in no way controversial. It is the clear meaning of texts both in St Paul and in the Gospels. This means that one ought not to bring any marriage to an end in order to embark on another. Only lifelong marriage can represent Jesus' teaching on the matter. But does it follow that, for a Christian, a final separation is *impossible*? Is there an absolute rule against it? Or (to put it in more technical language), is marriage 'indissoluble'? We have seen that, so far as scripture is concerned, there is no certainty that this was intended by Jesus. But it has been taught by the church for many centuries, and is believed by many Christians today. I have argued that it is at least doubtful whether the doctrine is supported by scripture; but there are other reasons for which it is held to be true. We shall not have done justice to it until we have looked at these also.

First we need to be clear what it means to say that marriage is 'indissoluble'. In one sense this is plainly untrue. Marriages are dissolved every day, at the rate (it is reported) of four in every ten of the marriages that take place in England; and many of these are marriages that were solemnized in church. What it *could* mean, of course, is that marriages *ought* not to be dissolved. From a Christian point of view, this is plainly as true as the literal meaning is untrue: Jesus was against divorce, and so should we be. This is the 'weak' view of indissolubility, and there is no great problem about it. But it is not what is in most people's minds when they say that marriage is indissoluble. They mean that a marriage once entered into (and consummated) *cannot* be dissolved. It creates a relationship which persists in some invisible way even if the couple no longer live together, are divorced and have entered into second marriages with other partners. It may *seem* as if the first marriage has come to an end. But this is an illusion. It continues to exist until the death of one of the partners. Divorce and remarriage are therefore not just wrong: they are impossible.

Compared with the 'weak' view of indissolubility, this view is a very strong one indeed. Yet it is the view which has been traditional in the church for a very long time, and it is important to see what it involves. In a society where divorce is infrequent and remarriage can be strictly controlled, it may not create too many problems. Those whose marriages fail and who are forced to separate are prevented by social and religious, or even by legal, prohibitions from marrying again, and society is able to contain and support the unhappiness and tensions which result. This was certainly the case when the doctrine was first accepted in the Middle Ages and is still arguably the case in the Republic of Ireland today. But when divorce reaches the proportions which we now see in most developed countries, the consequences for any church which continues to hold the 'strong' doctrine are, to say the least, uncomfortable. If it is believed that in any properly conducted and fully consummated marriage a spiritual or metaphysical link is forged (technically known by the Latin word *vinculum*, meaning 'bond'), a link which cannot be broken except by the death of one of the partners, it follows that those Christians (and there are many of them) who do in fact divorce and contract a second marriage are doing something highly irregular in the eyes of the church. It makes no difference if they are genuinely convinced that the first marriage in each case was a purely human mistake, in no sense intended by God, whereas the second is happy and apparently blessed. The church must still refuse to solemnize it or even to recognize it as valid, and may refuse full rights of membership (including communion) for many years thereafter. In their consciences the couple may be certain they have done right. But in the eyes of the church they are unrepentant sinners: the first marriage, being 'indissoluble', makes it impossible for the second to be officially acknowledged.

It is obvious that this position has become a very difficult one for the church to hold today. The church is supposed to welcome sinners, as Jesus did. It finds itself surrounded by thousands of people who hold the Christian faith and who have committed the particular sin of divorce. Many of these people are crying out for help and support, and the pastoral heart of the clergy longs to give it. But — either by church authorities or by their own conscience — many of these clergy are prevented from doing so. The doctrine of indissolubility makes it impossible either to recognize a second marriage or to welcome the couple fully into the fellowship of the church. It should be a very well-founded doctrine indeed which forces Christian ministers into such apparently un-Christian attitudes. If there turn out to be cracks in the foundations it will be hard to justify continuing to profess a doctrine which leads to such a large measure of suffering, embarrassment and pretence. We have already seen that the foundation in scripture is insecure. What about the other arguments which are appealed to?

The first arises directly from the passage in Genesis which we were considering in the last chapter: 'the two shall become one flesh'. When we ask how this would have been understood by Jesus' contemporaries, scholarly research gives us some significant answers. It was by no means always taken to refer to sexual union: 'one flesh' suggested kinship as much as it suggested intercourse, and it certainly was not felt to imply that marriage is indissoluble, since the society which devoutly believed the Bible to be the word of God also freely practised divorce. This does not mean, of course, that Jesus could not have taken it in a different way. He certainly used it as a reason for saying that divorce is wrong, and the surprise that this caused suggests he was doing something new. But we have seen that neither St Paul nor the author of Matthew's Gospel believed that Jesus had forbidden divorce and remarriage as an absolute rule; in which case they cannot have thought that the one-flesh passage, or Jesus' interpretation of it, made divorce *impossible*. In other words, I have argued that indissolubility does not follow necessarily from scripture.

This does not prevent us ourselves, however, from taking the Genesis passage to refer to the sexual union of man and wife and asking whether it is not as a matter of fact true that their intercourse creates a relationship that can never be broken. It can be said that the sexual act unites two people in a way that nothing else can; that those who experience it together enter a depth of mutual sharing greater than anything that is possible in a non-sexual relationship; that (at least if it is undertaken with real love and commitment) they will both be changed by it; that it is utterly unique, since the same act with a different partner will be a different experience; and that the profound relationship created by it is something which can never be made to be as if it had never been. The couple are marked by it for life. Nothing can efface it or 'dissolve' it.

Something important is certainly being said here, something which is at the heart of the Christian understanding of marriage. When a man and a woman are deeply in love, when they are resolved to share their lives and their very selves in every way, and when this mutual commitment is sealed, strengthened and enriched by their physical union, a relationship is formed which, though it may develop and change and be expressed in different ways over the years, is proof against any weight of responsibility or attack of adversity and fully justifies the vows of lifelong fidelity which are made at the moment of marriage. Moreover, so deeply does this relationship enter into the personality of wife and husband that both become different people. It becomes true to say that it *cannot* be brought to an end. It is a proper metaphor to say they are 'one flesh'. There is nothing that can make them cease to be so.

This, of course, is an ideal situation. It is what marriage, according to the Christian understanding, ought always to be. But suppose it does not work out like this. Suppose the marriage breaks down 'irretrievably'. Are we to say that the fact that the couple have been sexually united creates a bond between them such that they are bound together for ever and can never have another partner? There may seem to be some support for this in the emphasis placed by the law on a marriage being consummated. If there has been no physical union between the spouses the marriage may be annulled – i.e. regarded as if it has never taken place – and this has always been the case in the eyes of the church as well as of the civil law. This might suggest that sexual intercourse is what really makes a marriage: once it has taken place, the partners are changed people, bound to one another for ever. But if we say this we are getting this aspect of marriage out of proportion. Consummation is by no means the only factor. It may be a necessary one if the question is raised whether a couple is truly married. But other factors are necessary also – the free consent of the parties, for example. Neither in law nor in Christian teaching is the sexual union regarded as what actually constitutes marriage. But this still leaves the question whether it may not be the fact of the sexual act having taken place which creates the indissoluble bond. If this were so, of course, it would apply to every act of sexual intercourse, before and outside marriage as well as within marriage itself. It would mean that a man or a woman was indissolubly united with his or her first sexual partner: any subsequent relationship would be adulterous. To avoid doing what is forbidden everyone would have to marry the first person with whom they had had intercourse. In an ideal world, again, this might make good sense. Everyone ought to be chaste unless or until they are married, after which they can have no other partner (unless the first partner dies). But in the world as it is the results would be bizarre. The church could solemnize the marriages of only a small minority of those who applied. The rest – the great majority – would have to be regarded as 'living in sin'.

Nor were things very different in the time of Jesus. Prostitution is 'the oldest profession in the world'. St Paul had to warn his converts in Corinth against it (I Cor. 6.15–20). When doing so, he quoted the same passage from Genesis, 'the two shall become one flesh'. He used the text (as Christians have properly done ever since) to insist that any act of sexual intercourse is a serious matter, involving a profound oneness of the parties to it. It must never be regarded as trivial, or as having no personal consequences; this was doubtless the way some of his converts were tempted to see it, just as people are encouraged to see it like this today by the commercial exploitation of sex. Resorting to a prostitute was wrong, because it involved bodily union with someone whom one may never see again. And the body, for the Christian, is more than just one's physical make-up. It contains and expresses one's whole personal being. The sexual act affects one right down to the level of the spirit. But at that level the believer is united with Christ. One cannot allow that spiritual union to be invaded by a casual relationship with a prostitute! But notice what Paul does *not* say. He does not say that the offender must marry the prostitute, or that he has committed adultery. He draws none of the practical consequences which would follow from believing that sexual intercourse creates an indissoluble bond. The danger of resorting to prostitutes, and the necessity, under certain circumstances, of divorce, he recognizes were facts of life for his congregations. Of course they were to be regretted and deplored. But he did not take the line that they had now become *impossible*.

We must now look at a different approach altogether. Instead of talking about marriage in general, let us concentrate on marriage in church – 'Holy Matrimony'. This is more than a ceremony carried out publicly by human beings (though it includes this). It is a 'sacrament', which means that God is involved. According to the Catechism in the Book of Common Prayer, a 'sacrament' is 'an outward and visible sign of an inward and spiritual grace'. When the minister is conducting the service which joins the couple together in Holy Matrimony, something else is going on at a deeper level. The service is a sacrament: God is at work creating a new situation. But a sacrament, being God's work, is permanent. No human agency can render it ineffective. This, then, is the meaning of Jesus' words, 'Those whom God hath joined together let no man put asunder.' A sacrament cannot be set aside by the will of human beings. Divorce is not just undesirable. It is impossible.

Notice that we have shifted our ground here. The argument based on 'one flesh' was aimed at any second union. Whether or not the couple stayed together was not in the terms of reference. The point was that the partners to the first union could not have any other sexual relationship as long as both were alive. But the sacramental argument is aimed at divorce itself. Does the fact that a marriage is performed in church mean that by its very nature it must last for ever?

At first sight this is a powerful argument. But there are difficulties. We have first to answer the question, Is marriage a sacrament anyway? If we go back to the Catechism, we find the question, 'How many sacraments hath Christ ordained in his church?' And the answer is, 'Two only' – Baptism and the Lord's Supper. Nothing is said about marriage, and nowhere in the marriage service itself is there any suggestion that what is going on is a 'sacrament'. However, the answer is not quite so simple. The mediaeval church recognized not two but seven sacraments, one of which was marriage. Some of these the Protestants at the Reformation regarded as having been corrupted in the practice of the church, particularly Extreme Unction. They therefore preferred to concentrate on the two 'sacraments of the gospel', those that were specifically instituted by Christ. But the Church of England did not formally claim that the others were not sacraments at all. When the Catechism speaks of 'two only', it goes on to say that these are the two that are 'generally' (i.e. universally) 'necessary for salvation'. The others are not specifically said *not* to be sacraments. And in the minds of many Christians marriage certainly appears to be a sacrament of some sort: something is going on at the spiritual level while the 'outward and visible sign' is being performed in church.

A new twist was given to the argument in the fourth century by St Augustine. In the fifth chapter of the Letter to the Ephesians there is a powerful passage about marriage which we must return to in another connection. It ends with the words, 'This is a great mystery, signifying the union betwixt Christ and his church.' The Greek word for mystery is *mysterion*, which has a rather subtle meaning. When a writer uses a sexual analogy to convey his meaning, he has to be careful that he is not misunderstood. When Bishop John Robinson, in the Lady Chatterley's Lover case, called sexual intercourse 'an act of holy communion' it was more than many Christians could stomach. He might have done better to call it a 'mystery', meaning that you have to be prepared to take the analogy seriously, and avoid ribald comments about it, if you are going to see the point.[1] However, when the New Testament was translated into Latin (the text used by Augustine) the word chosen for *mysterion* was *sacramentum*. Augustine seized on this to prove that marriage is a sacrament. If so, it is like baptism. A person who has received baptism can never become un-baptized: God's grace in the sacrament can never become of no effect. So with marriage. The sacrament, once effected, is permanent. No marriage properly performed in church can be dissolved.

This argument has, to say the least, some weak points. First, and most obviously, *mysterion* does not mean 'sacrament'. It was a misleading translation in the first place that made the whole argument possible. Secondly, the passage in Ephesians is not about the marriage ceremony: it is about the whole life of the married couple. If there is anything 'sacramental' about marriage, it must be looked for (according to this passage) in the conduct of married life, not in the actual moment of getting married. And, thirdly, the argument, even if correct, is double-edged. If the minister at a marriage service is administering a sacrament, it does not follow that it can never be annulled. The church was given the power 'to bind and to loose' (Matt. 16.19; John 20.23). If it can bind a couple together in the sacrament of matrimony, it surely also has the power to release them from it. This is the view which has been taken historically by the Orthodox Church: under certain circumstances divorce is authorized by a priest, who is invoking the power of the church to loose as well as to bind. But the Western Church followed Augustine, only introducing certain refinements, such as that the efficacity of a sacrament requires that the persons are baptized: unbaptized people could therefore have their marriages dissolved.

In its strong form, then, this argument too has shaky foundations. But this is not to say that marriage is not a sacrament *of a kind*. The

Roman Catholic Church itself has recognized that sacraments are not all of equal importance. The fact that marriage is in some sense a sacrament need not imply that, like baptism, it can never be undone. Absolution from sin may also be a sacrament: but the forgiveness of God of which it assures us neither prevents us from sinning again nor can it be taken for granted (unless we repent) next time we sin. A Christian certainly wants to believe that God is at work when a marriage ceremony is performed in church, and may express this belief by saying that marriage is a 'sacrament'. But it does not necessarily follow from this that marriage is 'indissoluble'.

The third argument we must consider is of a different kind again. Marriage is often called a 'contract'; and this is what it is. Two people have 'contracted' a marriage; and in law we know what that means: both parties are under obligation to fulfil the contract made between them so long as the contract is in force. But this is not all that a marriage is. If it were, the parties could presumably terminate the contract just by agreeing to do so. In fact, however, the law does not allow this. Once married, the couple must remain married, either until one of them has died, or else until a further legal process has taken place which releases them from the contract and apportions responsibility for any obligations their marriage has incurred, particularly with regard to children. Their contract, in other words, is for life; and this is made plain to them whether they are married in a registry office or in a church. In the eyes of the law it is 'indissoluble' except by further legal action.

But there is more. At their wedding the couple do not simply sign a contract. They say words to each other which, by being said, create a new status for each. Just as the words 'I launch this ship', along with the breaking of a bottle of champagne and the working of the mechanism that lets it slide into the water, do actually mean that at a certain moment the ship is 'launched', so the pronouncement of certain words by the couple at the right moment under the right conditions means that they are at that moment actually married. And the form which these words take is that of a *vow*. The Prayer Book speaks of a 'vow and covenant betwixt them made'. This vow, again, is for life – 'as long as we both shall live' – whether it is a civil or church marriage. But the church service rams it home by adding 'for better or for worse, for richer for poorer, in sickness and in health'. Now a vow is a serious matter, all the more so when it is pronounced in church in front of a large gathering of people with all the solemnity that goes with a service which invokes the blessing of God. Does not the very utterance of such a vow commit one irrevocably for life? If there is the slightest risk of not being able to keep it, would it not be wiser (as the disciples suggested to Jesus in Matt. 19.10) not to get married at all? In other words, does not the vow itself make the marriage indissoluble?

What is a vow? According to the dictionary it is 'a solemn engagement, understanding or resolve to achieve something or to act in a certain way'.[2] It may be made to a god, in which case I may expect divine punishment if I break it; or it may be made to a human institution ('I vow to thee, my country') or to another person. The clear implication of any such vow is that I have every intention of fulfilling it and will so far as possible allow nothing to prevent me. Even if the object of the vow offers to release me from it (if my country does not need me any more) I shall still feel obliged to fulfil it.

This is certainly something much stronger than a promise. It is a bad thing to break a promise, but not necessarily that bad. It may be something I promised lightly or absent-mindedly, and now find that I cannot do. I may have promised to take you for a drive in my car and then found the battery was flat. It may be that when it comes to the point you do not want to go for a drive anyway. Many things can come between a promise and its fulfilment, and not keeping a promise is by no means always something one should be blamed for.

But a vow is a different matter. One should not make it if there is a risk of not being able to carry it out. The story of Jepthah in the Book of Judges (11.30–40), who had to kill his daughter because he had vowed to sacrifice the first living thing he should see when he came home after his victory, is a tragic example of the strength that a vow can have over one's better judgment. Jesus was highly critical of vows which could be used as pretexts for not fulfilling other duties (Mark 7.9–13). It is because a vow is such a serious thing that it must be taken so carefully. Once it is made it cannot be unmade. It binds the person who made it unconditionally. And if vows are solemnly made at the moment of marriage, does this not make marriage indissoluble? Who are lawyers to set aside such an absolute obligation?

But circumstances may change. It may become literally impossible for a vow to be fulfilled. I may vow to serve my country, but if I become totally disabled or find myself in prison I simply cannot fulfil

[2] *Shorter Oxford English Dictionary*

my vow. It occasionally happened that a husband was captured in war and sold into slavery in a distant country, with no expectation of ever seeing his wife again. He could not fulfil his vow. Did it make any sense to say that he was still bound by it? Alternatively, it may be possible to be released from a vow. A subject may vow allegiance to the king, the king may abdicate or be deposed, and release his subjects from the vow. Some of them, it is true, may not wish to be released and continue to feel bound by the original vow; but most will accept it and transfer their loyalty, with a new vow, to the king's successor. However binding the first vow, it is still possible to be released from it.

Philosophically, then, we may say that vows, though deeply serious and normally binding absolutely, may on occasion become impossible to fulfil, and release may be given. Does this apply to the vows of marriage? Are there circumstances in married life which make the vows literally impossible to fulfil? Here there is disagreement. Some would say that the couple have pledged themselves to each other 'for better or for worse'. They may find the going hard, they may turn out to be incompatible in various ways, they may inflict terrible hurt on each other. But none of this need make the fulfilment of their marriage vows literally impossible. With God's grace they may find means to bear their difficulties together, to be reconciled despite their differences, to forgive each other despite the depth of their wounds. To speak of 'impossibility', according to this view, is sheer faithlessness. Others would regard this as hopelessly idealistic. Love can die, interests can fly apart, personalities can become unbearable to each other. Marriages can break down irretrievably. Immense hurt and suffering can be involved in a vain effort to hold them together. The vows have become impossible to fulfil. Surely therefore they cannot still be binding?

The same kind of disagreement attends the idea of a 'release' from vows. In theory this sounds more promising. But we have already seen that husband and wife cannot simply release each other from their vows. The vows were made publicly, and created a new situation in law; and the law has to be called in if the parties are to be released. If the marriage took place in church, the vows were 'witnessed before God'. What human agency could offer release? Possibly the church; and it is true that in the past the church has assumed the power to release from other vows – those of monks and nuns for example. Certainly the Orthodox Church seems to do this when it 'looses' couples from the sacramental bond of marriage (though it might use other terms to describe this). Could not the Western Church do the same?

Possibly it could; but there is disagreement once again over whether it would be right for it to do so. Some would say that this would far exceed the powers of any church. The vows were made before God, only God can release from them – what God has joined together let no man put asunder. Moreover the Lord of the church is Christ, who was opposed to divorce. The church would be failing to uphold his teaching if it knowingly made divorce an option for a married couple. And anyway, what would its reasons be? That the vows had become impossible to fulfil? But this was the point made earlier on this side of the argument: it is never the case that to continue a marriage becomes utterly impossible. To allow any circumstances whatever to be a reason for release would be the thin edge of the wedge. If a marriage becomes 'impossible' in this case, why not in another? Even a slave held indefinitely apart from his wife in another continent should not be released from his vows. Who can say that in God's providence he may not one day gain his freedom and be able to rejoin her? Meanwhile those on the other side will point once again to what they see as the facts. Marriages do break down irretrievably. It can become literally impossible for spouses to continue with their marriage. To insist that they must continue to fulfil their vows may create untold suffering, out of all proportion to any good that could come of it. And in any case a part of their vow was 'to love and to cherish' their partner. Love cannot be commanded. If it has died, it becomes impossible to fulfil this part of the vow. Surely realism, as well as compassion, must compel the church to release them under these circumstances. And surely the Lord would not have withheld the power to do so when so much good might come of it?

Conducted in these philosophical terms, the outcome of the argument is clearly indecisive. Neither side can claim to have proved its case conclusively. Moreover, although all these discussions claim to be on matters of principle, it is noticeable that practical considerations tend to creep in. The question at issue is whether marriage is 'indissoluble' in the strong sense, i.e. whether, once contracted, it exists for ever (or at least until the death of one of the partners). Is there some continuing relationship that is created by every marriage (or at least every marriage solemnized in church), or some change produced in two persons by their sexual union, which makes a second marriage literally impossible? Such questions should be handled as objectively as possible. But in fact subjective arguments keep making their appearance. Those on one side have asked whether the strict view of indissolubility is 'realistic' or 'compassionate'; those on the other side have argued that for the church to release couples from their vows under certain circumstances would be 'the thin edge of the wedge', and so forth. As I admitted might be the case when we were discussing the evidence of the Bible, there is a danger of concentrating on just those arguments which support the conclusion one wants. Once again I am not claiming that I can clinch the matter. It will be sufficient to have shown that no one can be forced to believe that a marriage, even if solemnized in church, is (in the strong sense) indissoluble.

There are of course other ways of arguing the case for indissolubility. Suppose, for example, that a couple over a long period experience the joys of married life and successfully discharge its obligations. While they are doing so their lives, their emotions and their very thoughts become intimately enmeshed; all kinds of subtle and often unconscious bonds are formed between them; at times they may speak and think and feel for each other. Suppose that, later in life, they start drifting apart and then divorce and remarry. It would not be appropriate to say that the first marriage had come to an end. Both are different people from what they would have been if they had not been married to one another. Their relationship, having been so close and intimate, cannot suddenly cease to exist. It will continue in some sense even when each has remarried. From a personal and psychological point of view, we might well say that their first marriage was 'indissoluble'.

There is certainly some truth in this. Indeed it is important to recognize the extent to which married life is capable of making two people act as one and of knitting their two lives together in a subtle and complex way. Such a relationship cannot easily be 'dissolved'. But it would be unrealistic to suggest that all marriages are 'indissoluble' in this sense. For every marriage that achieves this depth of sharing and intimacy there is another in which the partners rapidly start growing apart. By no means all marriages result in a relationship deep enough to last for life. We cannot use this psychological model to argue for the indissolubility of marriage in general.

Traditionalists may of course say that all this is irrelevant. The church has a standard to proclaim and live by and has no business to compromise with a society which has adopted a lower one. The church is entrusted with the truth, and is simply being unfaithful if it tries to adjust this truth to the moral pressures of today. I shall be arguing later on that this is not the case. Christian understanding grows from a study of the human situation as well as of the Christian tradition. But in any case I do not believe that all the pressure comes from the world outside. If the arguments for indissolubility are not secure, there are important features of the Christian faith itself which make it vital to look at the question again. It is time to turn from these negative arguments about the possibility of bringing a marriage to an end and ask what positive things Christianity has to say about marriage itself.

4

'To Love, Cherish and Obey'?

What, then, is the positive teaching which Christianity has to offer about marriage?

We may begin with the one passage in the New Testament which tackles the matter in depth and which I have deliberately left on one side until this point.

> Husbands, love your wives, as Christ loved the church and gave himself up for it, to consecrate and cleanse it by water and word, so that he might present the church to himself all glorious, with no stain or wrinkle or anything of the sort, but holy and without blemish. In the same way men ought to love their wives, as they love their own bodies. In loving his wife a man loves himself. For no one ever hated his own body; on the contrary, he keeps it nourished and warm, and that is how Christ treats the church, because it is his body, of which we are living parts. 'This is why' (in the words of scripture) 'a man shall leave his father and mother and be united to his wife, and the two shall become one flesh.' There is hidden here a great truth,[1] which I take to refer to Christ and to the church.
>
> But it applies also to each one of you: the husband must love his wife as his very self, and the wife must show reverence for her husband (Eph. 5.25–33).

This is heavy theology; but not too heavy for it to have been incorporated in the marriage service of the Church of England. Indeed it yields an important insight into the nature of marriage. But for this to be understood a little introduction is needed.

The letter to the Ephesians is traditionally ascribed to St Paul. For the last two centuries scholars have been raising doubts about this, and today the majority view in the scholarly world is that Paul

---

[1] Literally: 'this is a great mystery'

himself is unlikely to be the author. Not that this affects its place in holy scripture. If it was not written by Paul himself it was written by someone close to him and incorporates many of his ideas. The church was not making a serious mistake when it placed it among Paul's letters. Paul taught and wrote far more than survives in the New Testament, and we need not doubt that his companions and followers gave a reasonably faithful account of his teaching, even if they no longer had his exact words. And the right way (it seemed to them) to get this teaching accepted in the church was to present it in the form of one of Paul's 'letters'. We do no dishonour to the result if we allow ourselves to doubt whether Paul was the actual author.

The passage we are concerned with stands in a sequence of paragraphs (5.21–6.9) each of which begins in a similar way:

Be subject to one another . . .
Wives, be subject to your husbands . . .
Husbands, love your wives . . .
Children, obey your parents . . .
Fathers, do not goad your children . . .
Slaves, give single-minded obedience to your earthly masters . . .
Masters, treat your slaves in the same spirit . . .

This is not very encouraging; indeed any sensitive person may feel embarrassed who has to read it aloud in church. It does not take long to notice that wives, children and slaves are told to be subject to husband, father or master, but the man in the house does not have to be subject to anyone! The household is utterly male-dominated and hierarchical. None of us would wish to see our homes run on these lines today (though some men might secretly wish they could be!), and even the most conservative Christians may have come to see that we cannot any longer use this passage as a model for family life, any more than we can still force a bride to say 'obey' in the marriage service. Not only does it presuppose a society very different from ours, it conflicts with hard-won values of equality between the sexes and mutual respect for dignity and personal responsibility which many of us feel are implicit in the Christian faith itself. How can we expect to find useful teaching about marriage in a text like this? Isn't it a world away from our social situation in the twentieth century?

But before we write it off there is something else to be noticed. The way the passage is constructed is not accidental. The headings are deliberate. Separate instructions are given to wives, husbands, children, parents, slaves, masters. This is a pattern which was quite often used by teachers of morality in the ancient world. They took a series of headings from the life of a typical household, and under each heading collected the teaching appropriate to it. Scholars call this pattern of moral instruction a 'household code'. There are examples of it in Greek, Latin and Jewish literature. And there is more than one in the New Testament.[2]

Suppose you want to write a simple manual on servicing a particular kind of car. You have to decide what order to arrange it in, and you are likely to look at other manuals to see how they do it. It will also make it easier for other people to find their way around your manual if they have got used to using others. This presupposes, of course, that all cars are built on the same general principles. The same kind of servicing procedure will do for this one as for others. The point of your manual is to help people to see where there is something particular about this car which is different from others and which needs a special servicing procedure. Where the job is much the same for any car – checking tyre pressures, for example – you need not spend much time describing it. You will concentrate on the things which are special to this one.

The so-called 'household codes' of the ancient world were, in effect, manuals of family life. Much of what they contained was standard moral teaching, the same for everyone: the teachers' main job was to make it attractive and memorable, so that, if you propped it up on your dressing-table, you might remember to put it into practice every time you felt angry with someone during the day. But each teacher who produced one of these 'codes' might also have something particular to say in it. He (so far as I know philosophers were almost always men!) could use it as an opportunity to give some special teaching of his own. You could never assume that every 'code' would say exactly the same thing.

This, at any rate, is what seems to be happening each time a 'code' appears in the New Testament. Under most of the headings the teaching in all of them is quite conventional. But in the two others (apart from this one) something particular is said about the relationship between slaves and their master which (especially in I Peter) reveals a new and important insight. And the same is true here. Under most of the headings the teaching is quite conventional and

---

[2] See Col. 3.18–4.1; I Peter 2.18–3.7

reflects the style of family life that would have been followed at the time by decent people anywhere (in which wives certainly had to 'obey' their husbands). But under the 'husbands' heading we get something quite new and (as it turns out) deeply Christian. And this, after all, is what we should expect. Jesus by no means covered everything in his teaching, and indeed (so far as we know) said very little about family life. But families in the new churches needed to know what style they should adopt. For the most part the only thing to do was to follow the highest standards that were generally accepted at the time. Much of the moral teaching in the New Testament letters is therefore quite conventional. But on some matters the new faith had something distinctive to say. Buried in the code one might find a jewel – or (more likely) an explosive charge!

We shall see later that this point is quite important for understanding Christian moral teaching in general. But for the moment it should warn us that we ought not to write off what our passage says about the nature of marriage just because it has buried it among some other pieces of advice which we can no longer find very helpful. We may always be in for a surprise; and in fact the section under husbands begins in a surprising way. 'Husbands, love your wives' – there is of course nothing surprising about that: it is what we would expect anyone to say, and the right way to put it in a Christian context might have been, 'as Christ loved us'. But what the writer actually says is, 'as Christ loved *the church*'. This, he says, is how husbands ought to love their wives. What does he mean?

I said earlier that this is heavy theology; but that does not mean it must be difficult to understand. It only means that there are one or two theological truths which have to be grasped first. One is that the church is 'Christ's body', an idea that Paul worked out on several occasions and which this passage takes for granted. Christian believers are bound together, and bound with Christ, at a deep level of faith and experience. Not only do they share each other's joys and sufferings, but Christ shares them also because in some sense what happens to them happens to him. You could say (this is one of Paul's ways of using the idea) that it is as if we are all parts of one body, each limb dependent on and affected by every other; and of this body Christ is the head. Or you could take it a stage further and say that we – the church – actually *are* Christ's body. A manner of speaking, of course. But one that expresses something absolutely real in Christian faith and experience. By sharing it we become more closely united with one another and so with Christ; by becoming united with Christ we become more united with one another.

A second theological truth is that Christ 'gave himself up' for the church. A Christian is quite used to the idea that Christ gave himself up for *us* – this is said many times in the New Testament, and usually means, 'for everyone', 'for the world'. That he did so for *the church* seems to limit the effect. But this is explained in what follows. We who are in the church respond to what he has done for us by being baptized, which means (in a sense) being 'cleansed'. We may go on doing sinful and morally dirty things; but by virtue of being members of this community of baptized people, God can regard us as 'glorious', 'holy' and 'blameless'. This may seem extraordinary language to use of people like us, who know ourselves (if we are honest) to be far from any such perfection. But again we can draw an analogy from experience. If we are deeply in love with someone, that person appears to us to have all the qualities just mentioned. In our eyes, he or she is perfect, wholly adorable. The daring proposition of the Christian faith is that this is how God sees us: he is in love with us. And the way he has shown this is by Christ having 'given himself' for us as a kind of sacrifice, not because anyone demanded it, but because this was God's way of expressing his love for us. Once we have seen and acknowledged this, and realize that it is not we who have earned it or deserved it but God who has created this new situation for us in sheer love, and once we have responded by accepting the 'cleansing' of baptism, then this theological language used about us – 'holy', 'glorious', 'blameless' – ceases to sound absurd. It is appropriate to Christ's body – which is us, the church.

So much for heavy theology. What has it got to do with marriage? The link is forged by the passage of Genesis which we have already spent some time over:

'a man . . . shall become united to his wife, and the two shall become one flesh'.

That is to say, it is as if husband and wife become parts of each other's body. We all take good care of our own body – 'we keep it nourished and warm'. This is how we are to think of a husband caring for his wife. But it is also a clue (if we can follow it: it is a daring, almost shocking, thought, which is why it is called a 'mystery') to the kind of intimate relationship and perpetual concern which exists between Christ and his church. We have just been told that the church is Christ's body. So the intimate relationship between man and wife can help us understand Christ's relationship with us, the church. Still more important: it works the other way round. It is by studying Christ that men can learn how to love their wives – 'love your wives, as Christ loved the church'. This loving involved Christ in utter self-sacrifice, giving himself to the church in such a way that she is cleansed, purified and perfected. Real love of one's body means bringing it to the best condition of which it is capable. Real love of one's wife means the kind of sacrifice of oneself which will release her full potential. And Christ's love for the church enables her – which means us – to become what we could never be on our own: 'holy and without blemish'.

We must not idealize this passage. A few verses earlier the author was using the church's relationship with Christ for a quite different purpose: to show that 'women must be subject to their husbands in everything'. And at the end, after repeating that 'a husband must love his wife as his very self' (which we can strongly approve of) he tells the wife to 'show reverence for her husband' – which is a polite translation: 'be in awe of her husband' would be a more accurate rendering of the original, and this most of us would equally strongly disapprove of! The writer has not been able to see beyond the limits of what was expected in any and every family that he can have known of. The husband and father had absolute authority in the household. Everyone else had to be subject to him. Any rebellious independence (and there must surely have been some) seemed a threat to social stability, and Christians felt they had as good reason to discourage it as anyone else. Then, as is often the case now, they felt bound to stand for traditional family values. It may not have occurred to them to bring Christian insight to bear on the place of women in the family, any more than it occurred to them to do so on the institution of slavery. But this did not prevent Christians from bringing the principles of their faith to bear on slavery many centuries later. Equally it should not prevent us from bringing them to bear on the place of women as well as men in the marriage partnership today.

For this is exactly what our passage helps us to do. The author has not taken an item of Jesus' teaching and tried to wring from it a rule about Christian married life (this is the procedure we were looking at in an earlier chapter). Quite possibly he did not know of any such item anyway. What he has done is taken some of the grand truths of

the Christian religion – that Christ loved us and gave himself for us,
that the church is his body which he cherishes in a deeply intimate
way – and applied them to the relationship between husband and
wife. The Hebrew scriptures which he knew did not say much about
this directly. The one text bearing upon it was the Genesis passage
about 'one flesh', which suggested at the very least that there should
be a close and constant intimacy between husband and wife. But in
Christ Christians now had a model of what that intimacy could
mean. Christ was as intimate with his church as a man is with his
own body. His relationship with it was expressed in a constantly
cherishing and utterly self-sacrificing love. From this one could read
off the quality of love a husband should have for his wife. We shall be
doing no more than following the same lead if we also read off from
it (as perhaps this author, as a man of his time, could not do) the
quality of love a wife should have for her husband. And there is a
further step which this writer took, and in which we should certainly
follow him. A couple which experiences this quality of love in their
marriage will be better able to acknowledge and understand the love
which Christ has had for us – which is one of the great affirmations
proclaimed by the Christian marriage service: through the love of
husband and wife we come to understand the love which God shows
to us in Christ, a love which in turn strengthens and enriches our love
for one another.

This passage, then, gives the Christian something positive to say
about marriage. But it also gives a valuable example of the *way* in
which to draw on our faith in order to tackle the problems we are
faced with today. This is so important that it is worth spending a
little time on it. The reader will have noticed that in discussing all
these matters I have been following a particular method. I begin with
scripture. But I do not believe this means just looking for texts with
which to support an argument. Before we can use any passage of the
Bible we have to know something of the context and circumstances
in which it was written. It may have been intended to answer a
question quite different from the one we are asking now. When we
have taken this into account, we may find that we cannot just apply it
to our own circumstances as if nothing had changed in the last two
thousand years. We then have to go behind this particular text and
ask whether there are any distinctive Christian principles expressed
in the New Testament which might bear on our question. Sometimes
there may be – and we have just seen a good example of this in the

New Testament itself. But often our questions have to be answered in more commonsense terms, without anything distinctively Christian being said at all. This is in fact what the church has been doing since the very beginning of Christianity. Before we go on to talk about marriage as it is today, it will be useful to study this question of method in a little more detail.

A good example is the passage from Ephesians which we have been looking at. Taken as a whole, it gives a great deal of advice which is not specifically 'Christian' at all; and the reason for this is that there were many questions which Jesus had not covered in his teaching but which the young Christian churches needed help with. Given that they had now adopted a new faith and in certain respects altered their life-style, there were many practical matters on which they needed guidance and on which Jesus appeared to have left no instructions. There were only two ways in which they could work out an answer to these questions. They could simply make sure that they did not fall below the best moral standards of the day; or they could look for principles in their new faith which might bear upon a particular moral issue and adjust their conduct accordingly.

We have examples of both these approaches in the New Testament Letters. For an example of the first, take the question, Should Christian ministers be paid by their congregations? An answer might be inferred from a proverb in scripture: 'You shall not muzzle an ox while it is treading out the grain.'[3] Or again: were Christians spending their time responsibly and keeping the right company? They should remember a Greek proverb: 'Bad company ruins good character.'[4]

It is not often that we get such direct quotations; but again and again we find that these writers were drawing, not on distinctively Christian teaching, but on a common stock of moral wisdom that can be found sometimes in Jewish and sometimes in Greek sources. Indeed in most respects the best moral standards of Jewish and Greek society were virtually identical and were supported by maxims, proverbs and moral reasoning that were common to both. Jewish writers on moral subjects were even known to pass off their compositions as the work of well-known classical authors. When a New Testament writer says something like 'children, obey your

---

[3] Deut. 25.4. quoted in I Cor. 9.9. and I Tim. 5.18
[4] A proverb from the Greek playwright Menander, quoted in I Cor. 15.33

parents' (Eph. 6.1–2) he may be inspired by one of the Ten
Commandments ('Honour your father and your mother'), by a
Hebrew proverb – 'My son, observe your father's commands'
(Prov. 6.20), or by one of the countless pagan maxims which tell you
to 'fear God and honour parents'. A great deal of moral wisdom,
then as now, was virtually universal. The task of these early
Christian writers was simply to remind their readers of it.

But there were also matters on which they felt they could give
distinctively Christian guidance. Slaves had to be obedient to their
masters. Everyone agreed about this, and Christians were not in the
business of inciting rebellion. But the example of Christ, who 'when
he was abused did not retaliate', gave a new dimension to the
undeserved sufferings which many slaves inevitably had to endure,
and a noble exhortation along these lines is worked into the
'household code' which we find in I Peter 2.18–25. Another instance
is the way Paul deals with the fact that he has heard of Christians in
Corinth going to law with one another (I Cor. 6.6–7). His first
reaction is to apply standard and generally accepted principles. No
community should let its internal quarrels spill over into the public
scene. 'Must Christian go to law with Christian – and before
unbelievers at that?' But then he suddenly stops short and asks
whether there is not a 'Christian' approach to it. 'Why not rather
submit to wrong? Why not let yourself be defrauded?' This is not far
from the ethic of the Sermon on the Mount, applied to a situation
Jesus would hardly have envisaged, but making good use of a
distinctive Christian principle to recommend what must have
seemed (as it still does) a radical style of behaviour.

Whether or not it has always acknowledged the fact, the church
has adopted much the same style of moral teaching ever since. No
one can suggest that Jesus left us a comprehensive guide to moral
conduct; indeed it is fairly clear that he did not intend to do so. His
teaching is questioning, challenging, sometimes daunting, occasionally enigmatic and almost impracticable – which is one reason why it
continues to haunt our consciences and inspire radically generous
and loving action in people two thousand years after it was given.
Anything more ordinary and more comfortably adjusted to our
normal standards and expectations would have been forgotten long
ago. Such teaching could never be systematic. It certainly was not
meant to cover every moral question of the time, let alone the new
questions which have been emerging ever since and which we find so

difficult today. But the church has been expected to help people with their decisions, to set moral standards and offer moral guidance. Where could it find the principles on which to do so? Sometimes a distinctive approach could be found implicit in a Christian doctrine. But for the most part the church did exactly what the New Testament writers had done. It borrowed from the best moral principles it could find in the world around.

These principles were not haphazard. It was not a case just of collecting everything one could in the way of good practice. The Greek and then the Roman civilization in which the church developed its thinking had a solid theoretical basis for the moral conduct it approved of. Ultimately many of its generally accepted principles went back to Aristotle. But in the Roman Empire there was just one school of philosophy which was generally regarded as sound and became virtually an established institution – Stoicism. We still say that a person has borne something 'stoically'. Sometimes we say 'philosophically', meaning the same thing. This is because for centuries Stoicism was *the* philosophy, and one of the things everybody knew about it was that it enabled people to bear suffering without being devastated by it – hence the word 'stoical'. The theoretical system which underlay this was an understanding of human beings whose destiny is to live in harmony with God and nature and whose ability to do so can be greatly strengthened by controlling physical appetites, emotions and passions. Not many people may have studied the theory; but a great many admired the results, and there were plenty of teachers and preachers helping people to see how foolish it is just to seek pleasure, worldly status and success. True happiness, they taught, is found in a more sensible, more 'philosophical' way of life.

The fundamental principle behind all this was that if you want to know what human beings *ought* to do (i.e. what is morally right) you can read it off from what they *are*. Apply your mind to nature – human nature, or the nature of the cosmos – and you can work out what to do. Much of it is common sense: you will find that most decent people instinctively do the same, whether or not they think a great deal about it. But if you want to be sure that your morality is soundly based, and if you want some moral principles to guide you in moments of difficulty, this is where you should look. And this is exactly where the church did look when it needed to work out principles to guide Christian people in all those areas of moral conduct where there was no obvious teaching of Jesus or Christian doctrine to appeal to. In due course this developed into a system called Natural Law, which draws much of its inspiration from Aristotle. But it is not difficult to trace its immediate origin back to that Stoic philosophy which was the framework for most people's moral upbringing in the Roman Empire and has left its mark even on the New Testament.

Natural Law is less talked about today than it used to be, though it remains the theoretical foundation of Roman Catholic teaching on moral questions. In the seventeenth and eighteenth centuries it came under formidable criticism from philosophers, who tried hard to discover a different basis for moral judgments; and in the twentieth century it came under attack also from Protestant theologians, who observed that it had not been strong enough to persuade many German Christians to condemn the atrocities committed by Hitler and argued that it must be replaced by an ethic that could be seen to be more directly in line with the gospel. In fact, however, it lives on as a moral guide to most people, though in a somewhat different form and under a different name: Human Rights. There is a wide consensus that human beings should not be tortured, deprived of life and liberty without due trial, discriminated against on grounds of sex, race or colour, denied the right to marry or travel as they wish, and so forth. These rights are based on fundamental principles of human dignity and equality, which are also a key element in the basis of Natural Law. The overlap is too great to be accidental. And historically it is possible to trace how one grew out of the other.

The essence of all this reasoning about moral laws or rights is the principle that the nature of human beings and of the world they inhabit, if properly understood, can tell us what we ought or ought not to do. For most of our history this has produced a fairly static morality. Throughout the Middle Ages there was little change in the way people understood either themselves or the world around them, and the moral laws which they inferred from this understanding of 'nature' remained much as they had been under the Roman Empire. The Renaissance certainly caused something of a revolution. The fact that the earth could be shown to go round the sun, that hitherto unknown continents had been discovered, that human beings had capacities undreamt of by their ancestors, meant that what was 'natural' had to be redefined, and philosophers began to doubt whether it any longer provided a basis for morality: that which lay in the *power* of human beings, rather than in their *nature* – their ability to choose what would give the greatest pleasure to the greatest number, for example – began to look like a more promising way of determining what one 'ought' to do. And the scientific and technological explosion of the twentieth century has called traditional moral rules more radically into question. To take only one example. In the nineteenth century it was still being taken for granted that the resources of the earth are there for us to exploit to our best advantage and that we can use and consume them in any way we wish. This was assumed to be the meaning of the promise in Genesis that human beings should 'have dominion' over all created things (1.26–29). Scientists should 'wrest her secrets' from nature, industry should extract all available mineral resources to bring wealth to the human race. Now all this has changed. An 'ecological' reading of nature yields a very different message. We should respect and preserve the earth's resources and limit our consumption for the sake of future generations. And biblical scholars are now telling us that this is a more correct reading of the passage in Genesis! Over quite a short period of history the rights and obligations that were read off 'nature' have changed fundamentally. The right to plunder has given way to the obligation to conserve. And both have been claimed to be in conformity with God's will as revealed in scripture.

But is this true of *human* nature? Men and women were made 'in the image of God'. God is by definition unchanging and unchangeable. So surely we must be the same. 'Human nature never changes' is a maxim not just of common sense. For a Christian it is surely guaranteed by the unchanging nature of God, in whose image we are created. But two qualifications need to be made. First, even if our 'nature' remains always the same it does not follow that we have always understood it correctly and inferred the right laws from it. Take the fundamental attribute of free will. It is certainly part of our nature that we are free to choose between good and evil. But it is also true that our freedom is curtailed by various factors outside our control. It used to be assumed that everyone is 'naturally' heterosexual. A homosexual was therefore called a 'pervert', on the grounds that he had deliberately 'perverted' his nature. There is now virtually indisputable evidence (which I shall be discussing later on) that this is not so. Some people are 'naturally' homosexual, and there is no way that they can alter the fact by an act of will. Indeed this must always have been so. What has changed is not human nature but our understanding of it: and the conclusions we draw from it about the moral implications of homosexuality are bound to change also. Other constraints on our freedom are revealed by psychology and the social sciences. A child that is deprived of a secure upbringing, loving parents and adequate schooling is simply not capable of responding with the same love and trust towards others as a child that has had a caring and stable home; it cannot be judged by the same moral standards. Both our genetic inheritance and our environment can affect our ability to choose the good. Moreover, our freedom of will is affected not just by what we cannot do but by what we *can* do. Women and men today have powers and opportunities undreamt of in former centuries. They can control the incidence of childbirth, mitigate the sterility of a marriage partner, detect deformity or disability in a foetus some months before birth or – at another extreme – risk the destruction of thousands of living beings, serious disability for future generations and irreparable damage to the environment by a single explosion. Human beings with these possibilities at their command can hardly be governed by exactly the same laws as were inferred from their 'nature' when none of these things was possible.

Non-Roman Catholics (and many Catholics) have been quick to see the implications of this when the question is that of artificial contraception. The papal teaching, they say, has taken no account of radically changed circumstances. The pressures of world population, the need to reduce the average size of families, and above all the new understanding of sexual intercourse as a precious means, not just of procreating children, but of deepening and enriching the relationship between husband and wife – all these are factors which fundament-ally affect the 'nature' of the most intimate part of married life. How can the traditional ban against contraception be maintained in the face of such a far-reaching change in understanding? As soon as the 'relational' value of sexual intercourse comes to be seen as at least as important as the procreative – as is almost universally the case today – it is hard to gain acceptance for the view that sex is right only when nothing is allowed to prevent conception. Nor need this be a case of a decline in respect for Natural Law simply because it stands in the way of something inherently pleasurable and which need have no undesirable consequences. It is rather that the 'nature' on which that law is based is now understood differently, and the persons to whom it applies have at their disposal means to cherish their most intimate relationship at the same time as exercising full responsibility over the size of their family. Consequently it can no longer be assumed that a law which is claimed to derive from their nature as created in the image of a loving God can properly exclude an activity of which the prime purpose is to cement their love for one another.

But the same critics of traditional Roman Catholic teaching (which was also that of the Anglican Church until it was decisively reversed by a resolution of the Lambeth Conference in 1958) are often slow to apply the same principles to other areas of family life. We frequently hear calls to the church to restore and strengthen 'traditional moral values', by which is often meant the pattern of family life which existed in former generations. But exactly the same arguments apply to this as to contraception. Were it still a condition of 'Christian' marriage that the wife should be 'subject' to her husband in the way intended by the passage in Ephesians – that is, staying at home to look after the household while the husband goes out to work, and leaving all decisions to him – how many people would get married in church? Equality of rights and opportunities for both sexes is something we have fought hard for; it is said by the Pope himself to be a key principle of Natural Law.[5] But this has consequences for married life. Brides are no longer required to promise to 'obey' their husband when their husband makes no corresponding promise to them, and few warm to the suggestion they should do so. To preserve this equality in marriage, wife and husband may properly agree that they should both continue their working careers, with only a brief interruption in the wife's case for starting a family. This will mean placing a strict limit on the time available for pregnancy, childbirth and looking after infants. It is from the 'nature' of these circumstances that the 'law' of married life has to be worked out today. It was from the experience of marriage in very different circumstances that the New Testament writers inferred the principle that wives should be 'obedient to their husbands'. Today we are bound to see the matter differently.

We return, then, to the question, What has our Christian faith to say about our marriages today? To answer it, the church – that is to say theologians, bishops, teachers and pastors – will need to begin by trying to learn from young couples themselves what the 'nature' of marriage is today. Marriage has existed for far longer than

[5] *Veritatis Splendor*, 1993, chapter 3, paragraph 96

Christianity and it flourishes in many places where Christianity has
no influence. Jesus did not invent any new form of marriage. The
only relevant story about him shows him attending a wedding feast
in Cana without any suggestion that there was anything in the rites
and ceremonies that he thought ought to be changed. Certain things,
doubtless, are constant – the exclusive nature of the relationship so
long as the marriage lasts, the responsibility of parents for the well-
being of their children (though the reciprocal responsibility of
children for their parents in old age has ceased to be taken for
granted). But there are also respects in which marriage has under-
gone significant change. Previously it was entered into as a matter of
course, under strong social pressure; now it is often freely and
deliberately chosen in preference to temporary or permanent
cohabitation. Previously it involved a clear division of responsibilities, the wife in the house, the husband at work; now the couple see
themselves as equal partners: both or either may be earning.
Previously the rearing of a family occupied most of the years the
couple could expect an active life together; now, with smaller
families and considerably longer expectation of life, they may have
many years before and after bringing up their children when their life
together will need to be based on other shared interests and
responsibilities. Until barely a century ago, mortality in childbirth
and the incidence of fatal illnesses meant that one marriage in three
was terminated by an early death and followed by remarriage; today
roughly the same proportion come to an end and are followed by
remarriage owing, not to death, but to divorce.

All this means that marriage is not, and cannot be, what it was.
Social and economic changes, many of which (such as equality
between the sexes and a lower mortality rate) Christians approve of
and may have actively worked for, have made it a more demanding
and often more deeply satisfying partnership. Its 'nature' is sufficiently different for the 'law' governing it to have to be looked at
afresh; and we shall need to ask what resources there are in our faith
for supporting and strengthening it. But before we start on this we
need to go back a little and say something about the couple's
relationship *before* their marriage. And this takes us into another
area where the church's traditional teaching leads to embarrassment
and pretence: the ban on all sexual relationships before and outside
marriage.

5

Sex before Marriage?

You are stately as a palm tree
and your breasts are like clusters of fruit.
I said, 'Let me climb up into the palm
to grasp its fronds'.
May I find your breasts like clusters
of grapes on the vine,
Your breath sweet-scented like apples,
Your mouth like fragrant wine
flowing smoothly to meet my caresses,
gliding over my lips and teeth (Song of Songs 7.7–9).

Many readers may be startled to find that this erotic poetry is in the
Bible. If so, they should read the so-called 'Song of Songs' from
beginning to end. They will find that it is nothing other than a piece
of exquisite and sensuous love poetry, often taking the form of a
dialogue between the lovers, expressing their longing for one another
and celebrating each other's beauty in terms of quite explicit sexual
attraction.

What is a poem of this kind doing in the Bible? In previous ages
this was hardly felt to be a problem. It seemed natural to believe the
meaning of the Bible lies deep under the surface. The plain meaning
of the text might be unimportant. To know what it was really saying
you needed to be able to de-code it. God would hardly have wanted
his people to see nothing in his sacred word but an excited
description of two lovers' feelings for each other. Clearly they stand
for something else. And for centuries Jewish readers have found in
this poetry a description of God's love for his people Israel.
Christians, similarly, have seen in it a statement of Christ's love for
his bride, the church. And the language is indeed so rich and
evocative that it has inspired a long succession of poets, philosophers
and religious thinkers to explore its infinitely suggestive symbolism.

This approach is not necessarily out-of-date today. The language of love has not lost its power to evoke the mystery of God's relationship with human beings, and the infinitely loving God who is at the heart of the Christian religion can still be adored and contemplated with the aid of language that may originally have been inspired by human passion. Yet few of us can now read the Bible in quite the way our ancestors did. Even if there are often deep layers of religious meaning in its stories and its imagery, we cannot help asking what actually happened, what the writer meant, and why he wrote it as he did. Old Testament narratives are not just improving stories (though of course they sometimes are): they purport to be historically true, and in many cases they can be checked against archaeological evidence or contemporary documents. The writings of prophets bear on particular historical situations, and our understanding of them is increased if we can reconstruct the circumstances in which they wrote. The author of the book of Daniel has assumed the character of a hero of the distant past; but critical study shows that he lived several centuries later, and we understand his work better, and receive more encouragement from it, if we can put ourselves in the shoes of its first readers and, like them, see cause for faith and hope under present trials in the miraculous deliverance of a man of faith in the past. And so it is with the Song of Songs. To learn all we can from it we need not only to see its possibilities as an allegory of divine love; we have to ask why the poem was written in the first place.

Modern versions of the Bible often try to answer the question for us. Recognizing that the poem is not a monologue but is a conversation between at least two speakers, they fill in the missing names. Some stanzas they give to 'the bride', some to 'the bride-groom'. This puts the poem at once into a well-known category, that of a 'wedding song'. Many of these have come down to us from the ancient world. They celebrate the moment when the bridegroom finally enters the bridal chamber for the night, and their subject is the excitement and joy which the couple experience when they are at last alone together. And indeed there are verses in the Song of Songs which fit well into this scenario:

Welcome King Solomon
wearing the crown which his mother placed on his head
on his wedding day, his day of joy (3.11).

We do not have to believe it was necessarily written for 'King Solomon', any more than we need ascribe all Proverbs to Solomon or all the Psalms to David. Solomon was known to be exceptionally wise; so a collection of proverbs could be valued as at least the kind of wisdom he was known for. He was gifted in composing songs (I Kings 4.32); so the Song could be properly placed under his patronage. We have a poem for a wedding (this time attributed to King David) in Psalm 45. If this is also the setting here, we can understand the apparently erotic language as perfectly proper in its place. It belongs to the ecstasy of the wedding night.

Yet it can hardly be said that the rest of the poem bears out this interpretation. In the first place, apart from the passage just quoted, there is no mention of marriage anywhere in the poem. Secondly, and more importantly, there are episodes in which something is happening which belongs to another world from the wedding feast:

> I opened to my love
> but my love had turned away and was gone;
> My heart sank when he turned his back.
> I sought him, but could not find him,
> I called, but there was no answer (5.6).

The girl is then apparently found wandering in the city in search of her lover, and is roughly treated by the watchmen. Clearly this passage is nothing to do with a wedding night. This part of the poem, if not others, seems to be what in later times would be the very stuff of romantic poetry – a description of a passionate love-affair, in which the lovers resort to every stratagem in order to be alone together. But were such amorous pursuits possible in the world of the Old Testament? And if they were, how are we to explain the fact that such an uninhibited description of them should have found its way into the Hebrew scriptures and have seldom aroused the smallest surprise or criticism?

To get these questions into focus we need to understand the social conventions of the time. Outside marriage and the family, how much freedom did men and women have to meet persons of the opposite sex? In the early days of a mainly rural society it seems that they had a good deal: women play a prominent part in many Old Testament stories. Later on, many parents may have been more protective of their daughters. But whatever degree of freedom was allowed, a heavy restraint on any form of permissiveness was imposed by the

law. Any girl found not to be a virgin when she came to be married
was liable to be punished by death (Deut. 22.20–21), and any man
who slept with an unmarried girl was obliged to marry her and to pay
a substantial sum to the girl's father (Deut. 22.28–29). As for
adultery, which is forbidden in the Seventh Commandment, any
proven case could be followed by the execution of both parties
(Deut. 22.22).

By the time of Christ these rigorous laws had been somewhat
softened in their application. The death penalty had ceased to be
frequently imposed, and a convenient legal loophole was found in
the difficulty of procuring witnesses to the act of adultery (this is the
background to the story of Jesus and the 'woman taken in adultery',
John 8.2–11) or indeed of any sexual offence – for the Jewish system
of criminal law always required that any charge should be supported
by the first-hand evidence of at least two witnesses. But one matter
on which later legal opinions were as insistent as the Bible was that it
was a source of shame, scandal and (for the girl's family) financial
loss if a bride were found not to be a virgin on her wedding night. For
the girl, the consequence of an indiscretion might be that the only
course open to her was prostitution; and for men, the legal
protection enjoyed by unmarried girls was a strong disincentive
against any sexual adventures other than with prostitutes. Prostitution was of course regarded as a social evil, but there is no doubt that
it flourished in both Old and New Testament times, and it was never
actually illegal. The Book of Proverbs contains numerous warnings
to young men against its dangerous enticements, and Jesus attracted
notice by deliberately cultivating the company of 'immoral women'.

Given a society in which there were such clear social norms, often
supported by legal sanctions, where should we look for a setting
appropriate to those passages of the Song which are clearly *not* part
of a wedding celebration? At least one such passage belongs to the
world of illicit and clandestine love affairs so familiar in modern
romantic literature:

> If only you were to me like a brother
>   nursed at my mother's breast!
> Then if I came upon you outside I could kiss you,
>   and no one would despise me (8.1).

Such poetry is timeless and perennial. No amount of repressive laws
or social conventions will eliminate these passionate adventures or

suppress the songs which they inspire. But before we jump to the conclusion that the whole Song is about this kind of intense but socially unacceptable relationship we must look at the rest of it; and it is clear for the most part that although the poem evokes, not the long-awaited security of the bridal chamber, but a series of emotionally charged encounters and the excited and intimate exploration of each other by the lovers, yet at times the relationship seems to be one that does not induce shame or require concealment. In short, the Song is an anthology of love poetry, ranging from bridal songs to secret serenades. The dominant impression is of a relationship which can only sometimes be acknowledged; for the rest of it has the drama and emotional tension of a passionate love affair.

Was there any situation in the ancient Jewish world in which such a relationship could have been regarded as sufficiently respectable for the poetry it gave rise to to hold its place so easily in holy scripture? – for it is very seldom in subsequent Jewish literature that we find any concern at the implications for public morality of these lyrical descriptions of sexual intimacy being found in the Bible. It is tempting to speculate that the situation might have been that of betrothal.[1] Marriages frequently took place when the parties were (by our standards) quite young. The moment of betrothal marked the moment when negotiations had been completed and a formal contract agreed between the families. If the couple were in love and became physically intimate, there would have been no legal consequences and only a certain degree of social disapproval if they slept together before the wedding. But this rather marginal bending of the social rules would hardly have been enough to make the poetry respectable. It is perhaps more realistic to look at it (as so often in the Bible) from the man's point of view. An affair with a Jewish girl was socially unacceptable and legally risky; resort to a prostitute was morally blameworthy and unlikely to arouse passion. But there was a third possibility. The Jewish law did not apply to slaves or foreigners. Relations with one of them would have no legal consequences or even attract great disapproval. In the song, the lady is dark-skinned (1.5) – certainly not a 'daughter of Jerusalem'! Her affair with a Jewish man need not have caused scandal and might have aroused such passion on both sides that it gave birth to this exquisite love poetry.

[1] As I have done rather rashly myself: *Theology*, Nov/Dec 1993 p. 462

But this is no more than conjecture. We are too far in time from the world in which the Song was composed to be able to do more than guess what occasions may have inspired its various parts. The mention of Solomon, his palanquin and his wedding day (3.7–11); the combination of urban luxury and rustic simplicity (3.8–9; 7.10–13); the dramatic pursuits and disappearances of the lovers; the suggestive imagery – all these may be literary conventions to which we have long lost the key, and prosaic questions about who the lovers were and what they were doing may be wide of the mark. But one thing we can say. Not only were these sensuous descriptions of physical passion deeply treasured in both the Jewish and the Christian religions for their power to evoke the blazing force of the love of God; the physical intimacy they presupposed was seldom subject to criticism or the cause of any doubt whether the poem should be part of scripture. This can hardly have been so unless occasions existed when such intimacy was not felt to be morally unacceptable. And we can say more. The poetry (for the most part) is certainly not about marriage and married love. The formalities of a wedding are never mentioned, and the relationship between the lovers has not yet acquired the steadiness and security which comes when they are finally committed to each other in marriage. Modern versions[2] which ascribe parts to 'bride' and 'bridegroom' are pulling the wool over our eyes: the original has no such stage directions, and these ones are appropriate only to a small part of the poetry. Yet the fact that fragments of a genuine wedding song do appear is significant. The bridegroom is 'Solomon'; and those who created the anthology apparently did not hesitate to include poems celebrating unmarried love alongside those which belonged to the public world of a royal wedding.

Since this is the one book in the Bible where anything is said directly about sexual love, it is worth spending a moment more on it to see how the writer approaches the subject. The first thing to say is that he (or, just conceivably, she) is extremely positive. There is no shame, no puritanism, none of that implied disapproval of the pleasures of the flesh which was so often expressed by later theologians. The physical beauty of the couple, as they appear in each other's eyes, is lyrically described, with delicacy but without inhibition. Secondly, the book gives no support whatsoever to the

[2] E.g. the Revised English Bible

doctrine which the church was later to make so much of that the prime, if not the only, purpose of the sexual act is procreation: the sexual attraction felt by these two lovers is never placed in the context of child-bearing – which is all the more striking in that this is a standard theme of wedding songs; indeed the fertility of a wife, and the duty to have a family, were matters that were regarded as of the greatest importance in the Jewish culture. In these two respects the approach is positive and affirming. Moreover, this frank celebration of the physical and (as we call it now) 'relational' aspects of love is nowhere contradicted in the rest of the Bible and should form part of any understanding of the sexual relationship which we claim is founded upon scripture.

So much for the positive side. What about the negative side? Isn't the Bible strict about any sexual permissiveness or abuse? There are certainly severe laws about any form of sexual behaviour which could have serious social implications, such as incest, bestiality or transvestites.[3] Above all there is strict prohibition of adultery and serious penalties are attached to it. The social consequences, in terms of the disruption of family life, could not be tolerated in such a close-knit and traditional society. What we do not find are any specific laws or injunctions against casual sexual relationships. But this is not surprising. As we have seen, the opportunities for such adventures were very few. No laws were required to restrain them. The only outlet for the licentious within the Jewish community was prostitution. This was legal: there is no formal prohibition of it in scripture. But young men were solemnly warned to avoid it,[4] and the word prostitute (or 'harlot') itself became one which was used by the prophets as a label for the religious faithlessness they abhorred – a usage continued by the author of the Book of Revelation when he wrote of 'the whore of Babylon'.

In this respect nothing had changed by the time of the New Testament. It was not necessary to utter warnings or lay down rules about casual or irregular sexual relationships in a society in which these things were socially unacceptable and could involve legal sanctions. But prostitution remained a social and moral evil against which Christians still needed to be sternly warned. 'Make no mistake: no fornicator . . . no adulterer . . . will possess the kingdom

[3] See Lev. 20.15,17; Deut. 22.5
[4] Prov. 7, and elsewhere

of God' (I Cor. 6.9–10). Given the social constraints which I have described, there can be no doubt that 'fornication' in this and all other passages where it occurs in the New Testament refers to recourse to a prostitute. Indeed, as we have seen, in 1 Corinthians 6 Paul speaks explicitly of 'one who joins himself to a prostitute'. His argument, based on the 'one flesh' text in Genesis, is that a Christian who does so is effectively involving Christ in prostitution, and is sinning 'against his own body' (6.15–18). If by 'fornication' he had meant a sexual relationship with someone who was not a prostitute – with a woman whom one hoped to marry, for example – the argument would not have worked. There would have been nothing wrong (on this argument) in 'taking parts of Christ's body and making them over to *a future wife*' – but this, of course, was not normally permitted by social convention.

We find, then, that the Bible is very strict indeed about adultery (which was a criminal offence) and prostitution (which was subject to strong moral condemnation) – though we have always to bear in mind that Jesus, in one well-authenticated episode,[5] refused to press for the judicial punishment of a woman allegedly caught in the act of adultery, and was frequently found in the company of prostitutes. This does not mean, of course, that he condoned these things. His message in each case was that such people should not be shunned but should be brought to repentance through kindness and understanding. But neither he nor the society in which he lived envisaged the possibility of sexual relations between respectable unmarried people, and it should cause no surprise that nothing is said about it anywhere in scripture. Not that sexual adventures of one kind or another were unheard of: the advice given to fathers in Ecclesiasticus and other ancient Jewish writings[6] to allow their unmarried daughters as little freedom as possible was presumably not unnecessary. Then, as at any period in history, there must have been young men about who were ready to seize a chance when they saw one. But the fact remains that the Bible does not explicitly condemn such behaviour. It did not need to: the social and legal constraints on it were already sufficiently severe.

Given, then, that the Bible says nothing about the degree of

---

[5] John 8.1–10. This passage is almost certainly not an original part of John's Gospel, but is usually thought to preserve an authentic tradition about Jesus
[6] Ecclus. 42.9–14; Pseudo-Phocylides (a Jewish collection in verse of moral instructions) 215–217

intimacy permitted in preparation for marriage, and given that the range of possibilities at different periods and in different cultures has extended from total segregation until the wedding day on the one hand to the cohabitation which is widely practised today on the other, where does the church look for support for its traditional teaching that all sex before or outside marriage is sinful? Clearly the question has to be widened. We have to ask what is the meaning and purpose of human sexuality in general: only then can we move to the particular matter of the circumstances under which sexual intimacy is appropriate. And the place to begin is, once again, those passages in Genesis which were quoted by Jesus and other Jewish teachers in connection with marriage and divorce:

> . . . male and female he created them . . . that is why a man leaves his father and mother and is united to his wife, and the two become one flesh (1.27; 2.24).

This time we are looking at them with another question in mind. What, if anything, do they tell us about the proper use and regulation of sex?

We have to be careful. This is a question which, so far as we know, no Jewish thinkers ever expected this text to answer. They did use it, certainly, to show that certain forms of sexual relationship were against God's will, for instance bestiality (the text is about men and women, not about men and animals) and polygamy (the text speaks of only one wife). They also occasionally drew from the story of the creation of man and woman the inference that they were intended for one another and that marriage would provide the 'partnership' which man needed (Gen. 3.18). But they did not go on from this to draw conclusions about the purpose of the sexual act itself. If we are tempted to do so today, we should be warned by the experience of Christians who, as recently as in the nineteenth century, found themselves in difficulties because they were trying to use the creation story in Genesis to answer questions of scientific cosmology. That story was never intended to give a literal account of the physical history of the universe. Even in antiquity it was realized that each 'day' of creation was a symbol for a much longer period of time (they thought a thousand years, we would say much longer); and the purpose of the story, though it makes use of cosmological concepts drawn from such scientific understanding as there was at the time it was written, was not to impart privileged scientific knowledge but to flesh out in narrative form the fundamental religious doctrine that God is the creator of heaven and earth. So with our passage about the creation of man and woman. There is no evidence that it was intended to answer questions about sexuality in general, nor was it read in this way by the ancient Jews. Its purpose was to show that marriage (implied by a man 'leaving his father and mother') was God's will for men and women from the very beginning. But even that conclusion needs handling with care. It tells us that marriage is the normal pattern for the relationship of men and women – as indeed is the case in virtually every society known to us. But it does not tell us that every man and woman should therefore conform to this pattern by marrying, any more than God's sentence on Adam that he would get his food 'only by labour' (Gen. 3.17) means that everyone (including, for instance, the disabled) should necessarily have to work. And those Jewish people (such as the community of the Dead Sea Scrolls) who opted for celibacy were not thought to be breaking the divine commandment to 'be fruitful and multiply' any more than Jesus was when he said that some might renounce marriage 'for the sake of the kingdom of heaven' (Matt. 19.12).

Rather, then, than to try to squeeze a complete doctrine of sexuality out of these passages, we should attend to what they do and do not say. They do say that men and women were made for partnership with each other, and that marriage is the normal form which this partnership takes. They do speak of man and wife becoming 'one flesh' in this relationship, which may reasonably be thought to refer to their sexual intercourse, though (as we saw earlier) at least one Jewish thinker took the phrase to mean family kinship. At least, therefore, this text may be taken to imply that marriage is the normal context for sexual intimacy just as it is the normal pattern for sexual relationships in society. But what is nowhere said in Genesis or anywhere else in the Bible is that the prime purpose of sex is the procreation of children. In so far as it is talked about at all, it appears as an important element in the marriage relationship and a strengthening of the partnership of husband and wife. The only reference to begetting children occurs in the command to the first man and woman to 'be fruitful and multiply' (Gen. 1.22; 9.7). This has always been taken by Jewish people to imply an obligation to raise a family. But, again, it is no more than a norm. Those who do not or cannot do so are not necessarily transgressing a commandment; and it would go far beyond the plain meaning of these words to say that they make procreation the only, or even the principal, function of the sexual act.

If it has not found the answer to its question in the Bible ('revelation'), the church has traditionally gone on to look for it in the way things are ('nature'). And at first sight biology appears to offer a much clearer answer than scripture. Biologically (and so 'naturally') there can be no doubt about the function of sex: it is to secure the continuation of the species through reproduction. But the act is also accompanied by intense pleasure: and for this also there is a 'natural' explanation. Child-bearing is a laborious and usually painful business. Other things being equal, human beings would surely avoid the pain (for the woman) and the consequent responsibilities (for the man and the woman) of having children. But nature has cunningly contrived to make the act that leads to conception so pleasurable that again and again men and women are tempted to indulge in it; and so the future of our race is assured.

This account of the matter is (as we shall see in a moment) absurdly inadequate, though it is not far from what I was taught when I was a boy by a bachelor schoolmaster. But it has always been a welcome account to those people for whom religion implies mortification and asceticism. I deliberately introduced the word 'tempted' at the end of the last paragraph. If the pleasure of sex is simply a means by which nature persuades us to do what we ought to do, then it must be a mark of a truly religious human being to be able to do without it, either by forgoing marriage and sexual relationships altogether or by enjoying it as little as possible within marriage. And look at the damage that yielding to this 'temptation' can do! Erotic desire can literally destroy the careers, the families, the very lives of men and women. Clearly any serious religious discipline should get these destructive urges under strict control. Marriage may involve the duty of procreation. But it is far better to resist the temptation of actually enjoying it!

It is easy to see that this view, even though it has been officially endorsed from time to time, is not only a long way from the much more positive approach to sex in the Bible; it is a misreading of the biological 'facts'. It is simply not true that no one would have children unless they were 'tempted' by the pleasure of intercourse. There is a deep urge in both men and women to found a family and to experience the joys and responsibilities of parenthood. Nor is it an adequate account of the pleasurable sensation of sex to say that it is only there to induce us to have a family. Modern psychology confirms what experience has always taught: sexual intercourse strengthens and enriches the relationship of men and women and unites them with a bond of shared emotional and physical experience which is unique to themselves and is an immensely powerful expression of their mutual love. To define it only in terms of the procreation of children is entirely inadequate. What is now often called the 'relational' aspect is at least as important.

Now clearly much depends on which of these aspects, the procreative or the relational, is regarded as the more important. If sex is defined primarily in relation to the procreation of children, this will affect our understanding both of marriage and of the place of sexual intercourse within it. The Book of Common Prayer was perfectly clear on the subject. In its Preface to the marriage service it placed the procreation of children first among 'the causes for which matrimony was ordained', and its only reference to the physical side of marriage was entirely negative: a means to avoid fornication. This was made somewhat less offensive to modern ways of thinking in the revised prayer book of 1928, but it was not until the Alternative Services Book of 1980 that a real change was made. For at least three hundred years, therefore, members of the Church of England heard a definition of marriage solemnly recited to them according to which the physical aspect had no honoured place other than as a means of bringing children into the world. It followed from this understanding of the matter that marriage must be the only context in which any sexual activity could be contemplated. The purpose of sex is to have children; children must be born within a marriage; therefore sex is confined to marriage.

This absolute priority given to the procreative over the relational aspect also affected attitudes to birth control. If the 'natural' purpose of sex is to procreate, then it follows that to indulge in it with the deliberate intention *not* to procreate is 'unnatural', therefore wrong. It is no accident that this was the official view of the Church of England and other Anglican churches until quite recently: church members who had again and again heard the Preface to the marriage service being read out in church could hardly have been expected to believe anything else. It is still also the official teaching of the Roman Catholic Church. But in this case there is a refinement. Although the 'nature' of the sexual act is held to be essentially procreative, it is observed that there are regular short periods in the monthly cycle when intercourse can take place but the woman cannot conceive. This biological fact can be read as a way of nature telling us that intercourse is sometimes right even when no conception can follow: there is a 'natural' form of birth control, such that at those moments it is not sinful for the couple to be united even if they do not intend to bring to birth a child.

All this (which can be traced back into the history of the mediaeval church and beyond) has now changed. The 1980 Alternative Services Book of the Church of England no longer gives priority to procreation in marriage: the relational aspect of physical intimacy takes first place, and is seen as an essential element of the deeply satisfying and challenging partnership of marriage, whether or not it results in the conception of children; and a similar shift of emphasis has taken place in most churches. Once again, this has important consequences with regard to birth control. Young married couples today are under strong moral and social pressure both to limit the size of their families and to plan the birth of their children in such a way that both have an equal chance to follow the career of their choice. In previous ages such a strategy would have involved long periods of sexual abstinence. Today it is made relatively easy by the means available for 'family planning'. These means imply, of course, that sexual intercourse may properly take place when it is not intended that a child should be born, and on these grounds artificial contraception is still prohibited by the Roman Catholic Church as 'unnatural'. But if it is granted that intercourse can bring about a precious strengthening and deepening of the relationship of the spouses, and that this indeed is one of its 'natural' functions, then there is no reason to say that it is 'unnatural' if there is no intention to procreate. Married couples may make love at moments of particular celebration or tenderness or relief, and in each case may deepen their love for one another by doing so. Along these lines it can be argued that such love-making is entirely 'natural' and is in line with the purposes that we can read off the facts of our sexuality. Indeed it may be said to be one of the most important achievements of modern technology that it has made it so easy for married love to be enriched in this way without placing a strain on the couple's obligation to plan their family and limit its size.

But a shift of emphasis is not a change of direction. If the emotional and affective − some would say even the spiritual − significance of sexual intercourse is at last being valued for what it is, that does not mean that we should devalue its role in procreation. On the contrary: it is this which still provides a vital key to understanding its place in the relationship of men and women. Every act of full sexual intercourse has the potential for resulting in the birth of a child. Whether or not the couple intended it – even if they deliberately tried to prevent it – it is always possible that a child may be conceived. It is this which gives to the act its seriousness and its mystery. The responsibility of bringing a new life into the world is one of the most solemn and demanding that we are given to bear. That a human being should be brought into the world by a kind of accident, as the unintended result of an experience sought for quite other reasons, is an affront to the value and dignity of the child and an abdication of moral responsibility by those who have so improvidently become its parents. Of course it is true that in the great majority of cases contraception will be effectively used and no birth will result. But unintended births are still by no means uncommon: it is estimated that nearly one in six of all pregnancies outside marriage end in abortion. Even if technology could offer impregnable security against unintended conceptions, we would still be bound to recognize that the act itself has this awesome potential, and the only way in which we can responsibly take this into account is by guaranteeing that if a child is born it will be received into a home loving and stable enough to give it a secure and affectionate upbringing. Traditionally, such a home has always been assumed to be provided only by marriage. It follows that it is only within marriage that sexual intercourse may be entered upon with full moral responsibility.

If this is the conclusion which follows on concentration upon the procreative aspect, the same goes also for the relational aspect. The more one sees the potential of sexual intimacy to reach the depths of the personality and to allow a couple to share a uniquely private and personal experience, the less it becomes possible to do justice to it in any context save that of a totally committed and exclusive relationship. Of course it is possible to argue that the importance of both these aspects can be exaggerated. Contraception can be virtually fail-safe; in which case the act ceases to have even the potential to result in a birth – which is of course the case anyway with an older woman, so why should it be 'unnatural' with a younger one? As for the depth of relationship involved, is not the most obvious feature of intercourse the intense pleasure which accompanies it? And since this pleasure is not inherently selfish (since it is shared), or socially harmful (so long as it is between consenting adults), and since it can be enhanced by being shared with different partners, surely it is perfectly reasonable and 'natural' that intercourse should take place far more widely than is allowed for in either Christian teaching or traditional social convention?

Certainly there is a school of philosophy according to which actions are right if they procure the maximum amount of pleasure and the minimum amount of pain. On this principle, it would seem that one could make a good case for a thoroughly permissive sexual ethic: any love-making must be good so long as it is pleasurable and so long as no pain or harm results from it. But in fact even the most single-minded proponents of Utilitarianism (as this philosophical view is called) have never thought in terms simply of physical pleasure. To do so is to believe in 'hedonism', which has never received moral or philosophical approval. They have preferred to speak of 'happiness', and have recognized that there is far more to this than what is ordinarily meant by 'pleasure'. If good acts are those which contribute to the maximum happiness, then all sorts of other factors have to be taken into account – emotional, psychological, even religious. And if we ask what makes people happy, we shall find a large number of different answers, ranging from faith and work to hobbies and humour. But one thing which is fairly constant in human experience as a source of happiness is the joy and security that comes from a deep and long-term personal relationship, enriched and strengthened by sexual intimacy and in many cases finding its most satisfying expression in the founding and bringing up of a family. Such a relationship demands total and exclusive commitment of the couple to one another. Any sexual adventure outside it is likely to be damaging to it, while the trust built up between them when they keep themselves entirely for one another becomes a vital ingredient in their relationship and enables them to engender love and confidence in others without arousing suspicion, threat or jealousy.

Thus it is not only religious asceticism or puritanism which frowns on sexual permissiveness: there are good philosophical grounds for regarding mere pleasure, and the absence of pain, as inadequate justification, on its own, for sexual intercourse. The 'nature' of the act itself, whether looked at primarily as procreative or as relational, seems to demand that it takes place within a loving, secure and long-term relationship such as is provided by marriage. This, at any rate, has been the traditional teaching of the churches, as of Judaism and Islam. The degree to which the physical side of marriage has been affirmed and celebrated has varied from time to time, particularly in the history of Christianity. But the necessity of a totally committed, exclusive and permanent relationship between the partners has been a constant in all Christian understanding of it, an understanding based on the nature of the sexual act itself and fully endorsed by all that can be found on the subject in scripture. One clear negative conclusion has always been seen to follow from this: no sex outside marriage!

Does this conclusion still follow? The fact that an argument is based on 'nature' does not mean that the conclusion will always be the same. Our understanding of the nature of human beings has changed in some respects significantly since rules of this kind were first formulated. We have seen already how there has been a shift of emphasis from that classically expressed in the 1662 Prayer Book (where the prime purpose of marriage, and so of the sexual act within it, was the procreation of children) to that of the 1980 Alternative Services Book where the 'joy of their bodily union' is said to 'strengthen the union of their hearts and lives'. This is the result, partly of a greater readiness in polite society to talk about sex as something positive and valuable in itself, partly of a great advance in psychological knowledge, based on empirical research, which has shown how deeply a sexual relationship can penetrate the personality and how profoundly it can affect and strengthen a personal relationship. But this is not all. Safe and painless methods of birth control have altered our perception of the nature of intercourse itself. Parenthood can now be planned and controlled to fit a strategy for giving both partners the best opportunity for fulfilling their potential in other spheres than domestic life; occasions on which a child is intended may be few and widely spaced. Moreover the couple must prepare themselves for the prospect (as it now is for most of us in developed countries) of many years of married life with no children to care for and therefore a greater need than in the past to strengthen their love for one another so that it does not depend too much on the shared interest of a family. In this, their sexual relationship takes on a new significance.

If our understanding of sex *within* marriage has changed and developed in this way, may there not be an argument for looking again at the possibility of a role for sex *before* marriage? If we now understand it primarily as a means of strengthening and enriching marriage, should we not also be ready to think of it also as a means of *preparing* for marriage? This, at any rate, is what a large number of people who come to the churches to be married are seriously proposing, and it surely deserves to be attended to. For, in effect, these same people have begun to take notice of the shift of emphasis I have been describing and to apply it to their own experience. The churches have been teaching for some time that the prime function of bodily union is to 'strengthen the union of hearts and minds'. Why should this wholesome process be confined to the years after the wedding? Is it not at least as valuable during the difficult time of courtship? The churches have also been publicly acknowledging that marriage today is a more difficult and demanding partnership than in the past; is it not all the more important to strengthen the relationship beforehand or at least to discover by experience whether there are hidden incompatibilities in this area of life which is now being said to be so important for the success of a marriage? In short, may it not be true to the nature of sexual intercourse to say that it is intended, not just for those who are married, but for those who are preparing for marriage?

If this were to be accepted, it would imply a further shift of emphasis: from procreative and relational to exploratory and pre-paratory. Once again, this does not mean that the former points of emphasis should be denied. The potential of every act of inter-course to lead to conception must still be taken seriously: there is no justification for it if the couple are not genuinely prepared to accept and rejoice in all possible consequences. The profoundly personal, emotional and psychological effects must still be taken account of. The word 'exploratory' is not a ticket for trying one partner after another until one finds the right one. It means exploring in this particularly deep and intimate way a relationship which is already on the way to becoming one of total mutual commitment. Of course the exploration may reveal unexpected obstacles; but these will have to be very serious if the marriage project of a couple who are in love is to founder on them, just as it has to be a serious and irremediable marital breakdown to justify divorce. But if the couple manifest the kind of commitment and fidelity to one another which we have seen to be demanded by the nature of every physical union, it is hard to see why arguments derived from this 'nature' should not extend to them as much as to those who resort to it to 'strengthen the union of their hearts and minds' in married life.

I have argued that there is no justification for regarding the Bible as negative and puritanical about sex. The Song of Songs is an uninhibited celebration of the physical side of love, and (like St Paul) stresses its relational function: the purpose of procreation is hardly mentioned anywhere. There are strict laws about sexual conduct which may be in any way socially damaging, particularly adultery, and strong warnings against making use of virtually the only opportunity for extra-marital sex, that is, prostitution. If nothing is said about casual sex, this is for the good reason that the situation did not arise. To form a judgment on the very different sexual conventions of today we need to supplement the biblical material (as the church has always done) with an understanding based on the nature of sexuality itself. This understanding has not always been the same. The almost exclusive emphasis which at some periods of church history has been placed on the procreative aspect has given place to a realization of its immense importance for the strengthening of the relationship between man and wife. This in its turn has entailed a radical change in attitudes towards birth control; and it is arguable that it should also be seen as a reason for considering whether sexual intimacy should be recognized as a legitimate part of the preparation for marriage between two persons whose love for one another is leading them towards total mutual commitment. If so, parish ministers might find that they could prepare couples for marriage a great deal more effectively. Instead of having to pretend they haven't noticed if the couple both give the same address, they could actually give some positive encouragement to them to use that intimacy as a serious way of preparing for the totally committed, exclusive and lifelong relationship which is what a Christian always means by marriage.

This conclusion may seem shocking to some traditionalists. Would not this be a fatal concession to the permissive society? If the church were to allow that under certain circumstances sex before marriage is acceptable, would it be long before *any* circumstances. were claimed to justify it? How could the church continue to stress the importance of restraint and fidelity if it openly sanctioned the opposite? To which the answer is, first, that this is already the situation. A large number of young people who come to be married are known to be living together, and it is sheer pretence to say that the church either does not know or forbids them to do so. Would it not be better (and far less hypocritical) to encourage the couple to see this experience as a genuine preparation for marriage? And secondly: the church could make a positive move that would show exactly where the boundaries lie. When a couple reaches the point of knowing that they are fully committed to each other, they could be offered a simple ceremony of betrothal. This would be on the firm understanding that they intend in due course to get married – though it would be only realistic to allow for the fact that an engagement, like a marriage, may result in failure and breakdown. Such a ceremony, undertaken in good faith and in the expectation of a subsequent marriage, would enable the couple to live together with a good conscience (if that is what they intend to do anyway) and the church to abandon its pretence that it knows nothing about it. It would not for one moment suggest that sexual intercourse is to be encouraged outside a relationship of total mutual commitment.

The same line of reasoning has implications for abortion. The debate on abortion tends to be conducted as a debate about conflicting rights – the 'right to life' of the foetus over against the rights of a woman over her own body. Certainly there are occasions when this language is appropriate. If the pregnancy is the result of rape, for example, the woman may justifiably claim the right to have it terminated. But what of a voluntary pregnancy? It is estimated that fifteen per cent of women who become pregnant outside marriage opt for an abortion. This can only mean that most of these pregnancies are unintended. In which case, can the woman still claim the 'right' to terminate it? With rights go responsibilities. If it is accepted that she has (in this sense) a right over her own body, the corresponding responsibility is that she should do her best to avoid the situation in the first place. Once the child is conceived, there may be strong arguments for abortion – the psychological health of the mother, the lack of provision for the child, the effect on an existing family. But to speak of a 'right' in this case is, to say the least, problematical. Pregnancy is not (normally) like a disability: we are not talking about the 'rights' of people who may be at a disadvantage through no fault of their own. It is the consequence of an act that may have been deliberately willed or willingly submitted to. The danger of talking about a 'right' to abortion, and of abortion being therefore easily available, is that it reduces the sense of responsibility which should go with any relationship that leads to sexual intercourse. The Christian view must surely be that this responsibility can be taken on only in a loving, stable and long-term relationship which is ready at any time to nurture a child that may be born.

6

Why Get Married?

'Why do you want to get married?' Until a few years ago this was hardly the question with which a minister was likely to begin an interview with a young couple who came to him to request him to marry them. They were in love – that was obvious. So naturally they wanted to get married. But today I would say that he would be foolish not to ask the question. Marriage is no longer the obvious option that it was. True, it is still popular: more than half the population prefer it. But an increasing number of people choose to live together without a formal marriage; and in some parts of Britain less than half the people who come before the courts with family problems are married. From the point of view of property, financial affairs or even social acceptability, cohabiting may seem at least as attractive. It saves the expense of a wedding. It avoids the legal delays and costs of a divorce if they decide to separate. So it is a real question: why get married? What has marriage got to offer that cannot be had simply by living together?

It is a question which church people cannot afford to ignore. Many of the young couple's friends may have opted for cohabitation. And their reasons may have been more than merely practical ones. Some may have ideological objections to marriage. If they have been even a little influenced by Marxism, they may see it as a means by which the capitalist system is sustained. Economic power in the conventional family is normally in the hands of the man, who is the partner who can use it most productively, there being no interruptions to his economic activity by reason of childbirth or domestic duties. Those young people (they are mainly young) who wish to protest against the values of a capitalist society observe the continuing domination by men of financial and industrial affairs and regard marriage as a sinister institution serving to perpetuate the economic system. Others may see it in more personal terms. Marriage is still weighed down by history and convention. It presupposes the dominance of the husband and reinforces an outdated subordination of the wife. True partnership and equality of the sexes is more easily achieved without the social pressures and conventional expectations which go with marriage. And in any case is there still good reason to insist on a relationship *for life*? When a couple has successfully brought up a family they may still have many years before them of active life. Is it necessary to continue with a union that has served its purpose and may become stale and quarrelsome? Why not enjoy the stimulus of a new relationship?

In the face of these genuine and reasoned objections to marriage, and in view of the fact that many couples deliberately opt for co-habitation, it will not do for the church simply to reiterate its traditional condemnation of any sexual relationship outside marriage. As we shall see later, some churches have already moved towards recognizing the validity of a long-term homosexual re-lationship, and it cannot be pastorally helpful to pretend that equally long-term relationships between men and women do not exist outside marriage. At the same time all churches have inherited a strong doctrine of 'Holy Matrimony'. Marriage, Christians be-lieve, is an institution 'ordained by God'. If they are to persuade others that this is indeed the best strategy for personal relations and family life, they must do this, not by declaring every other option to be sinful, but by demonstrating that marriage is still the way in which society is best served and individuals find their deepest satisfaction.

What, then, is marriage, and what are the arguments for entering into it?

At a certain point in the Church of England marriage service the minister solemnly recites to the congregation the exact nature of what the couple has just done. First, they have 'given their consent'. This is a fundamental principle in law as much as in the Christian understanding of marriage. Consent is at the very root of marriage. If either party enters into it under duress, it is not a true marriage, which is a union of two free individuals who have freely chosen to be united. The point was particularly important in earlier centuries, when a girl's marriage was likely to have been arranged by her parents. The service in the Book of Common Prayer deliberately gave the couple a chance to protest if either of them had been brought to the altar against their will. The priest solemnly abjured them:

I require and charge you both, as ye will answer at the dreadful day
of judgment . . . that if either of you know any impediment . . . ye
do now confess it.

There were of course other things which might constitute a legal
'impediment', such as a previous and undeclared marriage; and fear
inspired by the mention of 'the dreadful day of judgment' could lead
the guilty party to draw back in time. But the absence of free consent
could also render a marriage null and void, and this was the moment
to declare it. Times have changed since then, and not many people
are actually forced into marriage. The 'consent' of both parties can
usually be taken for granted. But there are still social and moral
pressures which may push people into marriage; there are unconscious impulses which may make someone desire marriage against
all better judgment. This is why it is so important to stress the biblical
understanding of marriage as a voluntary union of two absolutely
free persons. One of the ways in which a Christian minister can best
prepare a couple for marriage is by helping them to detect anything
which has constrained their choice and prevented them giving
absolutely free consent to each other. In this, law and religion are at
one. Consent in its fullest sense is the basis of marriage.

The second thing the couple have done is that they have 'pledged
their troth' or 'made their marriage vows' to each other. These vows,
as we saw earlier, are a serious matter. They are (whether in church
or a registry office) 'for life'; and a couple who are uncertain of one
another may feel that this is a sufficient reason for preferring not to
get married. But there is one ingredient in these vows which puts
things in a different perspective. This is what is usually called
'intention'. It is possible to make a promise but to have no intention
of fulfilling it. It is possible to make a vow, but to have all sorts of
inner reservations about whether one will regard it as binding in all
circumstances. As we saw earlier, there are vows from which it is
possible to be released, and it would be perfectly logical for a married
couple to make marriage vows to one another that were hedged
about with all sorts of conditions: 'I will . . . take you to be my
spouse, *so long as* you remain sane, faithful and reasonably
attractive to me . . . ' In this case, what would be lacking would not
be something in the vow itself but the intention with which it is made.
And for this reason the words of the marriage service make it
absolutely clear what the intention should be:

> . . . for better, for worse,
> for richer, for poorer,
> in sickness and in health,
> to love and to cherish,
> till death us do part . . .
> and this is my solemn vow.

As an intention, this is tremendous; and I do not doubt that most couples getting married will make the 'solemn vow' with absolute sincerity; a lifelong union for better or for worse is indeed their intention. But in other areas of life our intentions may change. I may firmly intend to become a doctor and believe that nothing will deter me from doing so. I might even say that I have vowed to spend my life in that profession. But later I may find that I can't stand the sight of blood, or that the necessary course in chemistry is impossibly difficult, and I shall not feel I have necessarily done anything wrong if I switch to training to be a maths teacher. In much the same way a newly married couple may find the going harder than they expected: they may find unexpected incompatibilities, they may discover they have few common interests, they may fall out of love. Wouldn't it then be natural for their intentions to change? Aren't they simply being realistic if they recognize that they have 'vowed' something which it turns out they ought never to have intended to go through with?

To answer this we need to look more closely at what is meant by a *marriage* vow. What is the nature of the 'bond' which the marriage vows create between those who make them?

In the Book of Common Prayer there is a phrase about vows which contains a significant word. Straight after the ceremony of marriage the minister refers to 'the vow *and covenant* betwixt them made'. The word 'covenant' is important in the Bible: it describes the relationship between God and human beings. It is not much used in common speech today; but there is a modern word which is virtually equivalent and which says a great deal about personal relationships: *commitment*. We can test the equivalence by trying it out on another familiar phrase. Christians call the Hebrew scriptures the 'Old Testament', their own scriptures the 'New Testament'. Here the word 'Testament' is the same in the original language as 'covenant'. If we now replace this by 'commitment' we get an exact description of what these scriptures are. The Old Testament is the story of God's commitment to his people Israel and the answering commitments which they were deemed to have made to him. On the people's side, this commitment was reneged upon many times: they faithlessly turned to other gods and were neglectful of the moral rules they had been given. But on God's side the commitment remained absolute and permanent. No matter what the people's failures, no matter how often they were disobedient, and despite the punishments and sufferings they brought upon themselves by their behaviour, God's commitment to them was unalterable, his relationship with them could never be broken. The New Testament carries this story into the new phase initiated by Jesus Christ. God's commitment is shown to be stronger even than all the forces of evil and the stubbornness of human hearts; and it now extends, not just to the Jewish people, but to 'all who call upon his name'.

It is a commitment of this depth and permanence which is evoked when marriage is called a 'covenant'. The couple are likely to *feel* totally 'committed' to one another at the moment of their marriage. The question is what happens if this feeling dies away: in what sense does their mutal 'commitment' (or covenant) still govern their relationship? To which the answer is that their feelings are not necessarily the most important thing. The difference between a commitment and an ordinary 'agreement' is that if one of the parties fails to live up to it or abide by it the commitment still stands. The ultimate model is the relationship between God and human beings. In this, it is by no means the case that we live up to what he expects of us. Again and again we fail and commit acts we are ashamed of. But this does not release God from his commitment to us. He continues to love us and to work through all the resources of his love for our ultimate good; we in turn come under the pressure of that love again and again to return to our commitment to him. And through this constant cycle of failure and renewal we find our relationship with God is deepened and strengthened. It becomes ever less conceivable that we can live in any other way.

We must of course believe that God's commitment to us has a firmness and a resilience that we can never approach. Our own relationships are bound to be a great deal more vulnerable and fragile. Nevertheless we can learn from it something of what the 'commitment' of marriage is intended to be; indeed in the experience of many married couples this is what it can be and is. It is the exact opposite of that experimental approach to relationships according to which the couple keep asking themselves and each other whether it is 'working out'. 'Commitment' means an absolute determination that it *will* work out. More, it involves living one's life on the supposition that it is worth any price to make it work out, and that nothing can happen which is serious enough to prevent it from doing so. The words 'for better or for worse' are not meant as a threat or a warning. The couple are not just saying that if things get tough they will take the consequences. They are entering into a commitment to each other which will certainly have its better and its worse moments, its joys and its sufferings, its quarrels and its reconciliations. But whereas in a simple love affair these moments may be taken as tests or symptoms of whether things are 'working out', the commitment of the couple to one another turns them into means by which their love is deepened and enriched. It isn't that their marriage *should* be able to stand the worse as well as the better. It is that the worse as well as the better is a necessary part of the experience they have vowed to share together and out of which they will build a still stronger union.

Consent, commitment. There is a third fundamental constituent of marriage, which is *witness*. The Book of Common Prayer puts it like this:

> . . . have witnessed the same before God and this company . . .

Recent forms of service may express it more simply: 'In the presence of God and before this congregation . . . ' But whatever the exact form of words, one thing is always made clear: marriage is not a private ceremony. It is here, perhaps, that some of the greatest difficulties are experienced today. We have been taught to think of most things that we do in very individual, not to say self-regarding, terms. And for a while a couple who are planning to get married may naturally feel that the only people really involved are themselves. The decision is one that properly falls on them alone. But as the wedding approaches they may find that more and more people are crowding on to the scene. First, their immediate families, who have an obvious stake in who their in-laws will be. Then a wide circle of friends, who are going to have to get used to a bonded couple instead of two independent individuals. Then (if it is a church wedding) the minister, other church personnel and even members of the local congregation who may want to show their support. From being a private matter it has gradually become a *social* one, in the sense that it involves an entire community. And the upshot will be a crowd of people in church for the service, whose presence is assumed in the wording, 'this company', 'this congregation'. What are they all doing there?

Not long ago I was present at a wedding in a large church. There were a great many people there, some from the local community, others from distant places. I was vividly conscious of what one might call the social power of the occasion – and the same is true of a wedding in the smallest parish church. The bride and bridegroom are the heroes of the hour, of course. But the others in the church are not just there to stare at them or throw confetti. They are there to show their support and affection, to pray for them, and to welcome them and integrate them as a new family nucleus within the network of a society of friends, neighbours and relatives. From this moment they cannot be alone, unsupported, uncared for; this support and care will be focussed on them *together*, and they in their turn, together, will be taking their place in this community of mutual support.

To some, all this may seem more of a threat than a promise. They had thought of a 'quiet wedding', just a few of their closest friends and family; and perhaps they will succeed in having it like that. But we are concerned, not with their personal preferences, but with the social consequences of any and every marriage. No one, and certainly not a married couple, can keep their lives entirely to themselves. And the presence of others at a wedding is not an intrusion on their privacy but an essential recognition that their consent and mutual commitment have social implications. On the one hand this is all to their advantage. However private they wish their life to be, there will be times when the support and friendship of others may be needed. So much goodwill, so many hopes for their happiness, such expectations of what the future holds for their married and family life – these are resources for their security and happiness which could be obtained in no other way. On the other hand, of course, something is demanded of them. By getting married they certainly acquire rights – the right to privacy together, the right to found a home and start a family, the right to be treated as husband and wife by society and by the state. But, as philosophers used to say, there are no rights without responsibilities. If they are to have these advantages by virtue of getting married, they must be willing to become part of the community which confers the same advantages on others. As friends, as neighbours, as citizens, they can provide the support and encouragement to others which flow from their own security in their commitment to one another.

It is this social dimension which is so often left out of the equation today when couples are debating whether it is preferable to get married or simply to live together. Granted that it is a decision that they have to make for themselves and no one can make for them; granted that the outcome will affect them far more deeply and decisively than anyone else; and granted that no one expects them to get married for any reason other than that they have deliberately chosen each other as their partner for life – yet marriage will always be more than a ceremony which puts a formal seal on their private intentions. It is a public act which gives them a new status in society and affects the entire network of their relationships with others. From this moment, everyone who has dealings with either of them – in friendship, in business, in social life, in law – has to recognize that the other partner may have a right to be consulted. 'I must ask my wife', 'I must ask my husband', is seen as an entirely legitimate step for a married person to take before making a decision. A consequence of marriage is that others can be expected to respect the union of wills that has taken place and to allow the couple space to reach a common mind on what they should do. In their contacts with others they are no longer two independent individuals. Even their working or professional lives cannot be entirely separate: employers or colleagues will acknowledge that a married person has to look after the needs and interests of his or her partner and may no longer be able to accept the same conditions and routine as a single person. All this follows from marriage. It may be that it is beginning to follow also from the simple fact of living together. An unmarried partner may receive the same kind of consideration as a married one. But in this case questions may be asked: is the relationship stable and permanent? Do the couple wish to be considered in the same way as people who are married? In order to extend its recognition and support of the intention of two people to form the kind of single social unit which is implied by marriage, society requires the assurance, either that they are married, or that they may be confidently treated as if they were. And the surest way to provide this assurance, and to receive the benefits which flow from it, is to get married.

Consent, commitment, the social dimension: we still have barely touched on the one vital ingredient of any marriage, which is love. It would be insulting to any couple who are in love with each other to suggest that there is something inferior about their relationship unless they get married, and still more insulting to claim they need to be Christians and to be married in church to understand what love is all about. Their love for each other may already have become something of great depth and intensity, and it would be impertinent to pretend that only marriage can guarantee that it will continue to be so. Yet Christianity, as I said at the beginning, is a religion of love. It proclaims a God whose very nature is love and who seeks a response in human beings of a corresponding love towards himself and towards one another. I believe that what it has to say about love is as crucial for marriage as it is for any other human relationship, and is the ultimate justification for the Christian insistence that marriage is the one fully satisfying framework and consummation of the love of a man and a woman.

'Thou shalt love thy neighbour as thyself.' There was nothing new about this when Jesus said it. It had stood for centuries in the Law of Moses as a fundamental moral commandment, and had often been taken to apply well beyond the bounds of one's actual 'neighbours'. Yet it had usually been understood to imply some restrictions. It is only human to love some people a great deal less than others, and there will always be some people so wicked or so totally opposed to us that we shall feel justified in not loving them at all. The originality of Jesus seems to have been that he removed all restrictions. Literally *anyone* may be your neighbour. And to make the point with brutal clarity, Jesus offered an injunction which is not only unprecedented as a piece of moral teaching but is demanding to the point (we tend to think) of near-impracticality: Love your enemy!

There is no doubt, therefore, that love – unconditional, demanding, totally generous – was fundamental to Jesus' teaching as well as to his living and dying. John's Gospel, which seems to report Jesus' words after they have already been subject to reflection and interpretation by his followers, gives the theme even more prominence: 'love one another' is a recurring motif. But the golden passage on love in the New Testament occurs, not in the Gospels, but in Paul. Confronted by the claims of the Christians in Corinth to have received extraordinary powers and gifts of the Holy Spirit, with the implication that anyone who could not perform these sensational feats of healing or speaking in tongues must be an inferior kind of Christian, Paul reminded them that the greatest of all gifts is love, which he proceeded to describe in unforgettable terms:

Love is patient and kind,
Love envies no one, is never boastful, never conceited, never rude;
Love is never selfish, never quick to take offence.
Love keeps no score of wrongs, takes no pleasure in the sins of
    others, but delights in the truth.
There is nothing love cannot face; there is no limit to its faith,
    its hope, its endurance (I Cor. 13. 4–7).

Stated as an ideal, this is challenging enough. We may well ask
ourselves from time to time whether our love for those we care for
comes up to this standard, and chide ourselves where we have most
obviously failed. But that is easily said in theory. The test comes
when we are sharing our life with someone else. When we have to
cope every day with the irritation, frustrations or sheer anger
caused by another person's habitual selfishness, infuriating habits,
occasional disloyalty – can we really say that our love 'keeps no
score of wrongs . . . there is no limit to its endurance'? There are a
number of situations which may expose us to such a test; that of a
son or daughter looking after an elderly parent, or a mother or
father with an apparently unmanageable child. But these, for the
most part, are temporary or at least relatively short-lived. The
parent dies, the child grows up, the situation changes. The one
context in which the test may be, by definition, long-term is that of
marriage. It is arguable, and indeed proved in the experience of
many married couples, that it is only in marriage that one can know
whether one's love for another person really has the quality which
Paul's words describe.

   They are words, of course, of faith. None of us knows whether
we are capable of a love which will survive all the testing that our
particular situation may throw at us. But they are also words of
experience. Such love exists: one has felt at least the stirring of it in
oneself and one has seen it in others. It is a resource of the human
spirit which God intends us to foster and be generous with, and we
believe it to have been signally embodied in the life and death of
Jesus Christ. It is the kind of loving, in other words, which is God's
greatest gift to us and which, in turn, brings us closest to God.
What it requires for its full development is a relationship in which
there is total and permanent commitment. There is literally no
human failing on either side which can extinguish it: 'there is no

limit to its faith, its hope, its endurance'. And the classic, and for many of us the only, situation of lifelong commitment, such that our love can be tested and enriched to this degree, is – marriage.

Love is a feeling, a powerful attraction of one person to another that looks for the response of an answering love. To this extent it is outside our deliberate will. We cannot be commanded to love what we find unlovable, we cannot be forced to respond to love which we find unattractive. But love is also action. St Francis found leprosy repellent until he engaged in the loving act of embracing a leper. We can all act in the way demanded by love long before any sentiment or passion impels us to. Similarly, the love of a married couple is not measured only, or even (after the early months or years) mainly, by the feelings they have for each other, but by the quality, the sensitivity, the generosity of their loving actions. Among these, most significant are their moments of mutual forgiveness and reconciliation. Two human personalities, however loving, will necessarily conflict from time to time. There will be anger, frustration, deep personal wounds. They may discover within their own natures that they have resources for remorse, forgiveness and renewed harmony, and they may experience the deepening which their love gains from the process. But the Christian religion, again, is about forgiveness and renewal. If we believe that God demands of us honesty about ourselves and a willingness to face up to what is wrong, to repent of it and to co-operate with the healing which he promises to us, then we find in marriage a privileged arena for experiencing the same cycle of forgiveness and renewal. It is the stuff of which an enduring love is nourished, and a pointer to the realities of our relationship with God. And, like love itself, it presupposes and flourishes in the total, lifelong commitment of one to the other, founded upon free consent and public acknowledgment, which is what the church has always taught marriage to be.

I have been suggesting reasons why a couple who feel fully committed to each other and intend to spend their lives together should opt for marriage rather than indefinite cohabiting. In part, my reasoning has been based (as before) on the nature of things as I understand them, in part (perhaps a greater part) on what I believe to be revealed in Christian faith and experience. To this extent, therefore, I do not expect my arguments to persuade those who are not Christians, or even all those who are. This is the way that I believe the gospel of love urges us to go, but that gospel itself does not carry all before it. Those who do not accept its truth need not accept the understanding of marriage it implies, though they must still attend to the common-sense and 'natural' arguments in favour of formal lifelong marriage – arguments which will be all the stronger when we come on to questions of family and the bringing up of children. Consequently, though I must strongly urge marriage as the right option, I cannot regard the alternative as sinful, any more than I can think it is sinful not to accept the gospel. I must either assume that the couple have not come to the Christian faith – in which case they are under no obligation to accept specifically Christian teaching about marriage; or else they are Christians who sincerely believe that they should not or cannot enter the commitment of marriage – in which case, so long as they are aware of all relevant Christian principles, I must respect their decision. But I shall continue, myself, to believe that marriage is the most satisfying and liberating option available to them, and shall endeavour to give this view credibility by witnessing to it, so far as I am able, in my own married life.

Much of what I have been trying to say has been based on the Bible; and it could be objected that I have twisted the evidence to suit my own purposes. We saw earlier that Paul is (to say the least) unenthusiastic about marriage: in view of an imminent crisis (as he believed) in world history he seems to have thought it better for Christians not to get tied up with it, and where he (or some follower) does talk about it more positively he is clearly thinking of a kind of marriage few of us would recommend today, where the wife is utterly subservient to her husband. I argued at that point that this is not the whole picture. There is one passage (in Ephesians) which gives us teaching which is positive and important; and the more negative-sounding passages are to be explained in the light of the circumstances of the time and the tradition of moral teaching that was available. Moreover there are general Christian principles in the New Testament which have a strong bearing on our understanding of marriage. But what about Jesus in all this? Is there not a strange silence about marriage in his teaching? And are there not at least hints that he, too, had a negative view?

It is certainly true that he does not say a great deal about it. There is the passage we looked at earlier, which was mainly concerned with divorce; there is the fact (according to John's Gospel) that he attended a wedding. He also used a wedding – a royal or wealthy one

– as the setting for a few parables. This does not amount to much; but then, what should we expect? Marriage, in his time, was taken for granted. It was a social institution which no one questioned. The question I have been concerned with in this chapter – why get married? – simply did not arise. There is no reason why Jesus should have said anything about it.

But there is one saying in Luke's Gospel which cannot be ignored:

> If anyone comes to me and does not hate his father and mother, wife and children, brothers and sisters, even his own life, he cannot be a disciple of mine (14.26).

This is a hard saying; and interpreters have tried to soften it. The first to do so may have been the author of Matthew's Gospel, where a similar saying occurs, but in a milder form:

> No one is worthy of me who cares more for father or mother than for me . . . (10.37).[1]

Commentators have been quick to suggest that this is what the harsher saying in Luke really means. In the Old Testament, 'Jacob I love but Esau I hate'[2] may mean no more than 'I love Jacob more than Esau'. The Hebrew idiom liked things in black and white: where we might say, I don't like him so much, they would say, I hate him. So Jesus may mean simply that we must love him more even than those dearest to us. But the fact remains that the text of Luke says 'hate', and includes a wife among those to be hated.

When applied to a wife or a member of the family, this sounds shocking; but I believe it is what Jesus intended. It would be entirely characteristic of him to have sharpened a point in his moral teaching by taking the extreme case and jolting us into attention by deliberate exaggeration. Of course we must love our wives and husbands, our parents and children. But Jesus issues a sharp challenge to our priorities. He has an urgent task for us, he invites us to adjust our lives to a radical programme. One of the easiest ways in which we can excuse ourselves from responding is by pleading 'family responsibilities'. In the case of a husband, the dictionary has a word for it: 'uxoriousness', which means failing to perform other duties because one tries to gratify every whim of one's wife. Clearly there is

---

[1] Matthew, unlike Luke, does not mention 'wife' at all
[2] Mal. 1.2, quoted in Rom. 9.13

a danger here, which Jesus characteristically exposes by his apparently brutal saying. 'You say you can't follow me because your wife or your husband won't allow it? Nonsense! The challenge is to everyone, the task is urgent, the call is pressing. There is no excuse for not responding, not even your wife, your husband or your family.'

In other words, the saying is not one that should be chalked up as a negative comment on family life, but as an invitation to put the whole matter in a larger context. In this chapter I have been affirming marriage warmly and strongly. I have used language about it which is appropriate to the noblest and most satisfying projects open to human beings. But it is not the highest priority of all. Our destiny (in the words of an old formula)[3] is 'to glorify God and enjoy him for ever'. Our human loves are to be taken up into a greater love that involves us in selfless service to others and constant striving for the values of God's kingdom. Marriage is a privileged means to this end; but at the end of the day it remains only a means. There are other paths through life which may be equally blessed, and Jesus himself taught that some may be called *not* to marry or have sexual relationships (Matt. 19.12). Marriage may afford the greatest happiness to two human beings. But it is also essentially a means by which they may give happiness to others. To this social dimension we must now turn.

[3] 'The Shorter Catechism', based on the Westminster Confession, 1648

7

Happy Families?

'Honour thy father and thy mother.'

It may come as a surprise if I say that this is the main thing the Bible has to say about family life. Christian leaders are fond of saying that 'the family' is a fundamental article of faith, and one would expect to be able to quote an array of texts to back this up. But in fact such texts are not easy to find. In Proverbs, sons are quite often told to be obedient to their fathers (e.g. 13.1), and fathers are occasionally told how to treat their sons (19.18); and the book ends with one of the most splendid descriptions of a housewife that can be found anywhere in literature (31). In the New Testament, Christian ministers are told that they must run their own homes properly (I Tim. 3.4, 12) (which tends to mean keeping their children in order), and wives that they must be obedient (I Tim. 2.11; Eph. 5.22). Children are told to obey their parents, and fathers not to provoke their children 'lest they lose heart' (Col. 3.21). Otherwise all we have is the somewhat daunting saying of Jesus which we were looking at a few pages back, apparently telling us not to let family ties be a pretext for evading the challenge of the gospel. As a basis for Christian teaching about the family, none of this seems to come to very much.

Once again, we must be realistic about what we ought to expect the Bible to have said on the subject. It was not necessary to tell people that a secure family life is important: this was taken for granted. And 'family life' meant more than the life of a home with two parents and one or two children. Families were (by our standards) 'extended' to include more than two generations and more than the very closest relatives. Indeed the word 'family' (in our sense) did not exist at all. One talked about one's 'house', and the typical family unit would be a household that might include servants and slaves as well as children and relatives. These households were the building blocks of society; any person's identity was tied up with belonging to one. There was no need for scripture to remind people of the importance of 'family life'.

It is all the more striking, then, that just this one aspect of family relationships (honouring one's parents) is included in the Ten Commandments. This was evidently not accidental. The same commandment is repeated, along with many others regulating social life, in Leviticus (19.3), and the punishment for a serious transgression of it was nothing less than death (20.9). Jesus also regarded it as of great importance, and sharply criticized some of his contemporaries for trying to evade their duty to their parents by pleading that religious obligations came first (Mark 7. 9–13). 'Honour thy father and thy mother' was evidently seen as a fundamental principle of family life. Is there any way in which it can still tell us something today?

We have to recognize, before we go any further, that our situation is very different from that presupposed in the Ten Commandments. It is not only that few of us have a neighbour who has 'manservants' and 'maidservants' (as is assumed in the Tenth Commandment); it is, quite simply, that we are likely to live longer than they did. Existing tombstones from the New Testament period show an average age at death of no more than thirty. Even if this is partly accounted for by the high rate of mortality at birth and in early youth, nevertheless it suggests that there was not a large number of old people around; and this cannot have been very different at an earlier period, particularly since young men would have been much involved in warfare. This makes it easier to understand why old people were felt to be worthy of particular respect. Not only might they be expected to have the wisdom of experience: there were not a great many of them! Hence the commandment, 'Rise in the presence of grey hairs, give honour to the aged' (Lev. 19.32).

By contrast, the different mortality pattern created by modern hygiene and medicine, combined with a much lower birth rate, has produced a quite different proportion between old and young. In most developed countries the old are on the way to outnumbering the young: 'grandfather' is no longer a rare survivor of a disappearing generation but a member of one of the largest classes in society – that of the relatively elderly. Nor does he necessarily gain respect by reason of his long experience of life. In former times he may have known a great deal that younger people did not know; but today the supply of knowledge is so great – from books, from the media, from experts – that his own particular wisdom may not be much in demand and is often actually obsolete. As for the social and economic links which bound the generations together, these have largely disappeared. Formerly a son or daughter depended on parents both for inheriting house, land or money and for acquiring traditional skills that would equip them for life. But now young people expect, and are expected, to make their own start in life without financial backing, and technology advances so fast that the knowledge and skills they need probably are not even possessed by their parents: they must get them from schools and colleges.

However, 'honouring' one's parents was never understood merely as a matter of respect and loyalty. It had practical implications. When they got old, parents would depend on their children for care and support. In large family units (and with relatively short life expectancy) this was not usually a problem: one could 'honour' one's parents in this way without too great a strain on the home. But modern conditions have broken this link also. The elderly can no longer live with their younger relatives, whose houses are inadequate and whose own families are too small and close-knit to bear the burden. The result is that after a certain age father and mother may have to be cared for by others, at their own or the state's expense. They may still be 'honoured' in the limited sense that their physical needs are provided for; but respect for them as a source of wisdom and knowledge, or even as a valued link in the family chain, has largely disappeared.

Those who clamour for a return to the 'basic morality' of the Ten Commandments should perhaps first reflect how far they believe that parents and grandparents should still receive appropriate 'honour'. They are unlikely to mean that small family units should once more begin to accept the burden of caring for aged parents or grandparents which may be crippling for their careers and stunting for their personalities. But it is important to ask why this duty of 'honouring' the older generation is singled out in the fundamental moral code of the Ten Commandments, whereas nothing is said, for example, about parents' obligations towards their children. Does it still have any relevance for us in the radically different social circumstances of today?

At the very least, it may help us to diagnose the sickness which is infecting a great deal of our family life. I said that 'honouring' was not merely a matter of feeling and dignity: it had practical implications in terms of physical and financial support. This was the point of Jesus' harsh words on the practice of avoiding obligations to one's parents by claiming to be putting one's money to a religious use.[1] One could go further, and say that, until recently, family life has been based on an unwritten contract. Children depended on their parents for their physical upbringing, their education and (in most cases) 'a start in life'. In due course, parents would come to depend on their children for care and support in their old age. In other words, each had an interest in honouring the other. If parents neglected their children they would not be able to look forward to security in later years; if children failed to respect and heed their parents, they could be punished by being expelled from the home or deprived of their inheritance and might lose the opportunity of learning the skills and knowledge they would need for adult life.

But now this contract has become virtually obsolete. Whereas in poor countries parents have children as an investment for their old age, in rich societies couples frequently say that they 'cannot afford' to have children. A high standard of living for all members of the family means that each child is seen as a considerable expense to the parents. Children come to be regarded as a financial liability rather than as a valuable security for the future. Moreover parents no longer have a material interest in their children making good. Their old age is likely to be provided for in other ways; and children who get the main part of their schooling and training outside the home and are expected to make their own careers for themselves have little reason to feel dependent on their parents other than for their basic physical needs. And there is a further factor which has loosened the ties of the contract. In the past, a child's values and standards of moral conduct, as well as a great deal of practical knowledge, were acquired from its parents. The only other important influence on its development was school, and what was taught in school was likely to be in tune with the traditional outlook and standards of the family. The generations remained bonded by the duty on one side of passing on inherited wisdom, skills and moral principles, and by the recognition on the other side that the family was the most reliable place to learn these things. But now there is an alien intruder in every family living room. We have become what sociologists call 'multiply resourceful'. Instead of the channels of information being confined

[1] The 'korban' dispute: Mark 7. 9–13

to home and school, with parents and teachers being able to control what was learnt, every family is now exposed to the much wider and more varied resources of television. Programmes are offered with a skill, an attractiveness and a persuasive power with which no parent can compete; and these resources give television an authority which the child or young adult may find more compelling than that of parents or school. It is estimated that an American child could have seen twenty thousand murders on television by the age of five. Even if British children are less dangerously exposed, they will still have seen a large number of violent deaths by the age of ten, along with orgies of destruction of physical property; by the age of fifteen a young person will have seen a similar number of unmarried men and women in various degrees of sexual intimacy. The screening of these things does not necessarily make them seem right; but their apparent acceptability on television, and the zest and abundance of resources with which they are shown, make it the more difficult for school and parents to carry authority when they say they are wrong.

In an ideal world none of this might matter. The moral values of parents could be relied on to exert the strongest influence on their children, and natural affection would guarantee cohesion and mutual respect in the family. But this is not how things are. Human beings are well endowed with selfishness, greed, ambition and cruelty. They are capable of lethal violence towards one another (as we see in the continual warfare that advanced international institutions are unable to prevent) and of wilful neglect of those entrusted to them. Just as warlike aggression has been restrained in the past, not by international laws and sanctions, but by the threat or use of answering force, so people's baser personal instincts have been restrained by the stake which parents had in their children's flourishing and by the gains which children might derive from attention to their parents. No one should be surprised by the consequences of these restraints being removed. We are not less selfish than we were; unless our natural affection for them is stronger, we may find that there are no longer any convincing arguments for preferring our children's well-being to our own. We are not less ambitious than we were; unless our ambition is transferred to our children we may find no reason not to resent the impediments which raising children may place in the way of our careers. We are not less pleasure-seeking than we were; without a real interest in the healthy development of our children we may be tempted to find our pleasure at their expense in ways that previous generations would have instinctively abhorred. That all this is the case is evidenced by a rising divorce rate, 'home-alone' children, homeless young people and wide-spread abuse. With the removal of social constraints and mutual self-interest, human beings require a strong moral motivation if they are to act responsibly towards those who are dependent on them.

Such motivation is of course present in a large number of people of differing religious faiths and of none. Christians have no grounds for claiming a monopoly of the good practice which exists in family life any more than in marriage itself. Many devout Christians will admit that they have failed to bring up their children as well as some of their non-Christian neighbours. Nor should we always assume that only the traditional family pattern of two parents and children in every home is capable of creating a secure environment for a growing family. In any case, this pattern is not as traditional as it sounds. Up to the end of the nineteenth century a great many mothers died before their children were grown up, most of them in childbirth. There were at least as many households with step-parents as there are now (though for a different reason). Moreover the typical family, at least until the Industrial Revolution, was much more extended than it is now, and was likely to embrace three if not four generations: the biblical command to 'honour thy father and thy mother' could be obeyed with much less strain on family life. It is also true – and moralists have no business to ignore the fact – that many single parents care for their children with a self-sacrificial devotion greater than that of many married couples, and the same may be true of couples who are cohabiting. Adhering to a 'traditional' family pattern does not guarantee the quality of family life; and in many cases that quality may be far superior in, say, a single-parent household than in the home of a married couple who are holding together 'only for the sake of the children'.

Given, then, that Christians – whether as individuals or as a church – should not rush into judgments about a family simply because the natural parent is single or cohabiting, we must still ask ourselves (as we did in the case of marriage) whether there are good reasons why we should continue to demand of church members, and seek to persuade all other parents or intending parents, that the traditional two-parent family is the option they should choose. It is, after all, no longer the case that the question answers itself. In our century, other patterns have been tried — the kibbutz in Israel, communal rearing in China — and children brought up in this way have not been less successful or well-adjusted to the world than many of those who come from 'conventional', but unhappy, families elsewhere. On what grounds should we continue to preach and commend just one pattern of family life?

To a certain extent we may find that most people agree with us anyway. There are strong commonsense reasons, backed up by psychological observation, for thinking that families in which husband and wife are together provide in principle the best environment in which children can be brought up and should be the norm in our society as it has been in the past. This, at any rate, is the view of adoption societies and has been reinforced by legislation. That is to say, where society has a choice over how children should be brought up (which it can exercise by regulating legal adoptions), it has opted for traditional two-parent families. Such a family is generally felt to be likely to provide the greatest emotional security for a child. Both mother and father appear to have an important role in up-bringing, and virtually every civilization of which we have any knowledge has taken this pattern for granted. Do we have to say any more?

Yes, I think we do. It is easy to say that human nature never changes, and that therefore something as basic as the relationship of a child with both its natural parents must always be preserved. But other things change; and it is quite possible that children in the future may flourish in a quite different family environment. The evidence of single-parent families themselves must be taken seriously. Over against the family of a totally united and stable marriage the children may be missing something; but in comparison with that of a selfish, quarrelsome and violent couple they may be better off; and the situation of a single parent may bring out qualities in her (it is usually the mother) of caring and unselfishness which might be slow to appear if there was a partner in the house. Certainly where there is a situation leading to divorce a child may grow up in much greater security if it is clearly in the charge of just one parent. Where there have been threats of domestic violence, it may be positively damaging to encourage the reunion of the parents.

But the changes I have in mind are at a deeper level than this. It is the role of the mother which is no longer the same. In virtually all previous ages it has been assumed (mainly by men) that a mother would be fully occupied with caring for a young child or children and running the home, and would be content to be so. But women's education, and the progressive opening of employment and careers to women, have called this assumption into question. Christians who have enthusiatically welcomed progress towards equality of the sexes cannot ignore the social consequences. If a woman has a right to earn a wage or follow a career she has a right to do so as an equal partner with men. It follows that she must be helped to make having children cause as short an interruption and as little disadvantage as possible. We would no longer think it right to oblige her to play the mother's role of a previous age – which would effectively mean leaving the world of work for at least ten years. So what is her role today?

There is no doubt that it has changed; and society acknowledges the fact. Governments have recognized an obligation to provide nursery schools. The arguments for these are partly educational: education can be extended back into infancy as well as forward into adulthood, to the benefit of the child. But in part they are social. 'Nursery education' is a means of enabling every mother to exercise her right to work. There may of course be some loss for the child in terms of emotional and psychological security; but the more 'educational' the 'schools' are, the more it can be claimed is gained in other ways. But this raises further questions. If we all generally approve of young children spending so many of their waking hours at 'school' rather than with their parents, and if this seems to have educational gains to make up for possible psychological and emotional losses; and if by this means women can increasingly take their rightful place in the world of work – then why should we not extend this further, and make arrangements to take babies off their mothers' hands just as soon as is practicable? May not the gain to the mother outweigh any possible losses for the child? And if both parents are likely to be out at work for the greater part of a child's early life, does it any longer matter so much what sort of 'family' it grows up in? Is it still realistic to say that the traditional two-parent family should be the norm?

All this is logical enough; but many people will instinctively draw back from the conclusion. Having children is a great deal more than tolerating an interruption to one's work. People want to enjoy their families, not just have them. Clearly what is at stake is not just a matter of personal rights and opportunities. Deeper values are involved. Children also have rights, and happiness does not derive only from individual freedom. One might think this would be taken for granted, and that parents could be relied on to do the best for their children. But even this is not necessarily so. To take one significant example: until the present time it has always seemed a natural ambition, both of individuals and of states, to ensure that the world will be at least as good a place, if not better, for our children to live in as we have had it ourselves. There has been a kind of unwritten covenant between the generations, such that it was always felt wrong to use up wealth and resources that should be preserved and passed on to the next generation. In return, the young owed respect and gratitude to their elders for the improvements they enjoyed. 'Honour thy father and thy mother' was a commandment with a clear rationale: it was to one's parents that one owed the assurance that one could expect to live and work in circumstances at least as favourable as theirs had been. In return, the parents had an answering responsibility: to make the best possible provision for the next generation.

This covenant, or mutual commitment, underwent an unprecedented weakening in the 1960s when a whole generation of young people came to feel betrayed by their elders. Far from inheriting a better world, they found themselves in one of staring injustice between rich and poor, north and south, and with humanity constantly threatened by the unimaginable horrors of nuclear war. Part of the motivation to 'honour' their parents seemed suddenly to have disappeared. At the same time it began to be realized that the prodigious technological advances of the post-war years involved hidden environmental costs that would one day have to be repaid. Meanwhile, with a falling birthrate, the burden of support of an increasingly long-lived older generation was going to fall on a diminishing number of younger wage-earners. Unsolved technical problems – in particular the safe disposal of nuclear waste – were being bequeathed to the scientists of the future, and the financial burden of remedying the massive pollution caused by their parents' generation would have to be carried by their children. Since then, in addition, it has begun to be realized that social welfare cannot be sustained for much longer at its present level, so that the next generation will receive less support from public expenditure: already young people are being placed in debt by being forced to pay back some of the cost of their education as soon as they begin to earn. In effect – and perhaps for the first time in the history of our civilization – the covenant between the generations is being broken. Instead of investing in their children, the generation of the parents is living on resources which will have to be repaid or repaired by the generation of their children.

In this and other ways it can no longer be taken for granted that parents will place the interests of their children before their own. The balance of rights and responsibilities has shifted significantly: parents are far more ready than they were to claim rights for themselves at the expense of those who are at present dependent on them. The pressure for nursery 'education' is only partly, and not always convincingly, claimed to be on behalf of the children; it often has more to do with the desire of the parents to be relieved of the burden of caring for small children. Once again we have an instance of the social constraints which up to now have held families together in a network of mutual interests being quietly relaxed. Whereas, before, the interests and well-being of children were clearly the responsibility of parents, now governments find it necessary to legislate to protect them. Whereas, before, it was normal for parents to be expected to make sacrifices for their children's nurture and education, now parents claim the right to be relieved of much of this responsibility and children are asked to 'pay back' some of the costs in order to maintain their parents' standard of living. Whereas, before, parents regarded the moral upbringing of their children as something for which they took personal responsibility, now they cheerfully admit a stranger into their home equipped with all the resources and techniques of the mass media: against the subtle and insistent persuasion of television programmes they can hardly expect their own relatively inarticulate values to prevail. Faced with such a widespread relinquishing by their parents of traditional responsibilities towards them, it is not surprising if the traditional response, 'honour thy father and thy mother', finds little purchase in children's minds.

Not, of course, that all these developments are bad. The sacrifices demanded by the family were not equally shared. The father was responsible for providing the money needed for family life and education, but the work by which he did so was usually what he would have done anyway, and his workplace was a valued part of his identity. The mother, on the other hand, was obliged to give up virtually all her interests and her independence for the sake of the home: where sacrifices have been involved, it has been mainly women who have made them. What we have seen in recent years is a long overdue redressing of the balance, and no call to return to 'traditional family values' should be responded to if it is merely a way of shifting the burden back on to women. My point is simply this: that these social changes, however much good they may have brought with them, have altered not just the normal pattern of family life but some of the fundamental assumptions which used to sustain it.

Given, then, that the question is not so much about social conventions and institutions as about the basic values and motivation which sustain any form of family life, it is reasonable to challenge the teachers of the Christian religion and ask what they have to say about it. It will not be helpful if they merely continue to repeat that the church must continue to support 'the family'. As we have seen, for most of the history of Christianity the family could be taken for granted. It is only now that the question is being asked whether it is really such a sacred institution, and there is disappointingly little in the Bible or in traditional Christian teaching which helps us to answer it. On the other hand there are at least two general – and, so far as we can tell, highly distinctive – principles which were insisted on by Jesus and which, if accepted, offer a strong motivation for parents to accept the commitment involved in having children and to adopt a secure and permanent style of family life. These are: the acceptance of children as an end and not a means, and a recognition of the significance of addressing God as 'father'.

First, Jesus' attitude to children. This is highlighted by two sayings in the Gospels:

Let the children come to me; do not try to stop them; for the kingdom of God belongs to such as these. Truly I tell you: whoever does not accept the kingdom of God like a child will never enter it (Mark 10. 14–15).

He called a child, set him in front of them, and said, 'Truly I tell you: unless you turn round and become like children, you will never enter the kingdom of Heaven. Whoever humbles himself and becomes like this child will be the greatest in the kingdom of Heaven, and whoever receives one such child in my name receives me' (Matt. 18. 2–5).

Anyone who has been in a traditional culture in the Middle East knows that there is no such thing as privacy. There are small children everywhere, and Jesus' open-air ministry will have attracted them all the time. They were an habitual nuisance (as children may be anywhere), and adults develop ways of greater or less severity of chasing them out of the way. People were certainly not sentimental about them – that is something that had to wait for the Romantic era of the nineteenth century. When philosophers and teachers talked about them at all, they did so entirely in terms of their potential. Children, they said, are a blessing, not because of what they are, but of what they will be. Have patience with them, and they will grow into something worth having in the end.

Of course it is risky to generalize. Many people must have enjoyed their children, as we do, for what they were and not for what they would one day become. But, so far as I know, no other teacher in the ancient world did what Jesus did, that is, use children as examples of what *adults* should become. No one else insisted, as Jesus did, that children deserved at least as much respect as anyone else – and this, not because they were valuable assets for the future, but because there is something in a child which is closer to the kingdom of heaven than all the alleged wisdom and maturity of the adult. He did not say – or rather, he is not recorded as having said – exactly what qualities he found in them which made him value them so highly. We must not attribute to him ideas, which are quite modern, about the innocence, spontaneity and freshness of small children. But we can look at it the other way round: we can read off from the Beatitudes some of the qualities of character which Jesus valued most highly. Blessed are the poor in spirit . . . those who can cry (the sorrowful) . . . the gentle . . . who have a passion for fairness . . . who show kindness . . . whose hearts are pure . . . who are peacemakers . . . Which of us adults can truthfully say that we are more likely to be these things than children are?

This then is our first principle, derived directly from sayings which bear the stamp of Jesus' originality. Children are not just an asset for the future, or a commitment to be undertaken for the sake of society; they are not just a problem or a responsibility (though they may be all these things). They are of infinite value *as children*. They deserve at least as much respect and care as any other human beings. Being dependent and vulnerable, they have an unanswerable claim on our concern and attention; and they have qualities which may bring them closer to the kingdom of heaven than a great many adults. It follows that Christians have a specific mandate to check the shift which seems to be taking place (if I have rightly discerned it) from an instinctive concern for the rights and well-being of children to a preoccupation with the rights and freedoms of adults and parents. A recall to 'Christian family values' should mean a challenge to do at least as well by one's children as all those parents (and thank God there are still many) who make the interests and healthy development of their children their very first priority, worth any self-sacrifice (though this must be shared between them) and sustained by a love that is stronger than any discouragement.

The second principle derives from a theme that is prominent right through the Bible: the fatherhood of God. This needs to be handled carefully: first, because there are dangers in attributing a human characteristic to God and then arguing that we ought to have it ourselves; and secondly, because it can so easily be used, as it has been in the past, as a way of giving religious sanction to a patriarchal mode of family life. To call God 'Father' may be no more than to project on to God what we think a father ought to be (usually from a male point of view) and then to fashion our human 'fatherhood' accordingly – leaving the equally important concept of motherhood quite out of the picture. But this would be a travesty of what the Bible has to say about God as 'father'. The idea, of course, was not unique to Hebrews and Christians. Other religions and cultures called God 'father', usually in the sense of creator and originator of the human race. But the Hebrews had a distinctive conception of the relationship of this God to his people Israel. As we saw when we were discussing 'covenant' or 'commitment', they experienced God as a being who had freely and deliberately bound himself to them and whose commitment to them could never be broken however miserably they, for their part, failed to keep their role of the covenant. To express this perception of divine commitment and responsibility, the prophets used the analogy of a father with his children. But in doing so they were not opting for the father's role as against the mother's. Indeed, from time to time they seem deliberately to use mother-language of God's 'fatherhood', ascribing to him emotions and concerns that are characteristically feminine.[2] It is clear that God's 'fathering' has little to do with paternity; it embraces

---

[2] Hos. 11.1–4; Isa. 49.15 etc.

a wider range of emotions and attitudes than would be characteristic of any human male. It would be nearer the mark to call it by the modern word 'parenting', with qualities and attributes that may be shown equally by a father or a mother. Far from being a projection on to God of a patriarchal mode of fatherhood, it was an attempt to find a human analogy for the constancy of relationship which this people had experienced in God. His total commitment to them was like that of a parent whose love and concern for a child could be extinguished by no discouragement.

This prophetic perception of God's inviolable relationship with his people being like that of a father with his children offers a model for human parenting. It is also endorsed and deepened by Jesus. Again, the most pregnant sayings about this occur in John's Gospel – not only does Jesus constantly address God as his father, but his enemies actually criticize him for 'calling God his own father' (John 5.18). Significantly, on one occasion, Jesus says 'I honour my father' (John 8.49), using the language of the Commandment to indicate how a natural and proper human relationship could validly point to a relationship with God. None of this may be quite as Jesus said it: John's Gospel, as I said earlier, seems to embody a stage of later reflection on the person and teaching of Jesus. But there is much that is similar elsewhere in the New Testament. Throughout all the Gospels Jesus calls God his 'father' and seems to have used a particularly intimate word – *abba* – in doing so.[3] Moreover he encouraged his followers to do the same (Rom. 8.15; Gal. 4.6), and taught them to pray 'Our Father'.[4] Everywhere we find the same conviction of God's absolute faithfulness, compassion and caring, directed now, not just to the Jewish people, but to all who call upon him as Father through the Son, Jesus Christ.

Here then is our second principle. Men and women are made in the image of God; and this image stamps their parenting – the moment when they share in the mystery of God's creation of the human race. It is a parenting that involves total commitment to the child, a shared commitment (since both parents are involved in the act of conception) and one that therefore must be worked out in permanent partnership. Of course things may turn out otherwise. One partner may conscientiously believe that she can fulfil her commitment to her

[3] Mark 14.36. Some scholars have suggested that this was as familiar a word as 'Daddy', but this is far from certain
[4] Or simply 'Father'; Luke 11.2

child only if she removes it from the tensions of an unhappy home or the negative influence of her partner. The principle does not impose lifelong marriage in every case where the parents have irremediably failed in their project of sharing their lives and responsibilities. Our religion (this is one of the themes of this book) allows for failure and has important things to say about it. But the principle is clear in what it says about the commitment implied by parenting. Both parents have an absolute responsibility for their child, one that no harshness of circumstances or waywardness of character can lessen. God's commitment to us is unbreakable; so is ours to our children. This responsibility is most naturally discharged in lifelong marriage. Even if this fails, the responsibility is still there: neither parent can cease to be responsible, the commitment cannot be reneged upon. There may, on occasion, be ways it can be exercised other than by the two natural parents living together. This has always been the case for a variety of reasons. But any form the commitment takes must be determined by the well-being of the child. Every personal preference has to yield to this priority – which is, after all, the principle which comes into play when a question of the care of children comes before a court. To be responsible for the children we share in creating is part of what it means to be created in the image of God.

'Honour thy father and thy mother' (Ex. 20.12). 'Fathers, do not provoke your children' (Col. 3.21). These two injunctions are separated by many hundreds of years. The first belongs to an early stage of Hebrew law and morality (in many respects similar to that of surrounding cultures), the second to a piece of Christian teaching which was of a piece with what was being urged on people by other moral teachers in the ancient world – backed up, in this case, by what looks like a bit of sound psychology: 'do not provoke your children *in case they lose heart*'. What they have in common is an insistence upon responsibilities – the responsibilities of adult children towards their ageing parents, the responsibilities of parents towards their young children. These responsibilities imply rights – the right both of the elderly and of children to be looked after and cared for. But this implication was not drawn in earlier times. The language of rights does not occur anywhere in the Bible, and it was not until many centuries later that the concept of rights as of something belonging to every human being began to be spelt out by philosophers and political thinkers. When this happened (principally in the seventeenth and eighteenth centuries) it was insisted that rights carry

with them answering responsibilities. But in the half-century
following 1945, during which human rights have moved high up on
the moral and political agenda, responsibilities have tended to be
neglected. I have suggested that we can see signs of this also in family
life. If so, perhaps the most urgent task for Christians and the clearest
mandate they receive from the scriptures ('Honour thy father and thy
mother'), is to alert people to the consequences of this subtle shift of
priorities and recall them (beginning with ourselves) to that profound sense of mutual respect and responsibility between the
generations which has been taken for granted through most of our
history. Whatever outward form family life may take today and in
the future, this must surely be the one factor which remains constant
and which can assure the well-being both of our children and of our
whole society.

All of which, of course, is no more than the framework for a rich
and fulfilling family life. Whether the promise is fulfilled will depend
on something much deeper. The same quality of self-sacrificing,
trusting and liberating love, which we saw to be Christianity's
greatest challenge – and, on occasion, gift – to marriage, is
demanded equally by family life. Those testing moments when
children are physically dependent on their parents to the point of
adult exhaustion, or when conflicts over training and discipline push
patience to the limit, or when young people have finally to be trusted
with their independence before they have the maturity to cope with it
– all these are sustained and enriched by the resources of forgiveness
and reconciliation, of faith and love, which are inherent in the
Christian faith. We must return to this before we end; but first there
is another form of intimate partnership that cries out to be
considered. Not all Christians, not all human beings, can or will have
a married and family life. It is time we attended to these others.

8

'This Man and this Woman'?

Jesus lived among people for whom marriage was taken for granted as the norm. Some religious teachers went so far as to say that it was an obligation for every man to marry. But Jesus himself (in all probability, though we cannot prove it) was not married. Nor was John the Baptist. Nor was Paul (though he may have been widowed). There were ascetic communities in Palestine and elsewhere of which the members remained celibate. So we need not assume that Jesus regarded marriage as obligatory. Did he have anything to say about people who could not, or preferred not to, marry?

There is one very striking saying attributed to him which takes us to the heart of the matter.

> There are eunuchs who have been so from birth, and there are eunuchs who have been made eunuchs by men, and there are eunuchs who have made themselves eunuchs for the sake of the kingdom of heaven (Matt. 19.12).[1]

I have deliberately quoted this in a version which translates the word for 'eunuch' literally; for it is this word which gives the saying its startling impact. Eunuchs were totally foreign to the Jewish culture. They were a recognized institution in some Eastern courts: they were believed to make particularly faithful ministers and servants (perhaps because they relied on their masters to protect them from public contempt). One of them appears as a visitor to Jerusalem in Acts (8.27). But castration deprived a Jew of all rights (Deut. 23.1), though the lawyers recognized that there were cases of men being sexually impotent from birth. Given, then, that Jesus can have meant by 'eunuchs' only a rare class of foreigners or the small number of his fellow Jews who suffered from congenital impotence, why did he

---

[1] Revised Standard Version. The Revised English Bible has 'those incapable of marriage'

bring them into the discussion of marriage? The answer appears to
be in the last clause: 'those who have made themselves eunchs for the
sake of the kingdom of heaven'. This has occasionally been taken
literally by Christians, thinking it was the right way to deal with their
sinful sexual impulses. But it is extremely unlikely that this is what
Jesus meant. It is true that in pagan religions there were instances of
people castrating themselves as a sacred duty. But anything of this
kind would have been so abhorrent to Jewish sensitivities that it
could hardly have been part of Jesus' programme for his followers.
On the other hand, what *was* characteristic of Jesus was to make a
point by a touch of startling, if not shocking, exaggeration. There is a
close parallel in the Sermon on the Mount. 'If your right hand causes
your downfall, cut it out and fling it away' (Matt. 5.30). This too has
occasionally been taken literally; there will always be extreme
ascetics and self-mutilators in every religion. But the meaning is
clearly metaphorical. Your 'right hand' is any priority or aptitude
that is leading you astray. And so it is here. 'Those who have made
eunuchs of themselves' are those who have made a voluntary
renunciation of sexual relationships.

But the fact remains that Jesus used a startling, not to say
shocking, way of making his point. The idea of 'making oneself a
eunuch' was both exotic and repellent. Jesus evidently had something arresting to say, and adopted a powerful image for saying it. He
introduced it, as so often in his teaching, by calling attention to
people who tended to be despised (impotent by birth) or who were
well outside normal society (castrated eunuchs). There was something about them, he suggested – and this was his originality – which
can teach us an important lesson. For the sake of the kingdom we
could even consider becoming (in some sense) like one of them!

Both the point of the teaching and the way it was expressed must
have caused surprise. In a society where marriage was assumed to be
the norm, deliberate renunciation of all sexual relationships could
hardly have been approved of – we know of it happening only in
communities which set themselves apart from normal society; and
the use of the word 'eunuch' in this context would have produced at
least a certain *frisson*. But it was not long before it was eagerly taken
up by the church as an endorsement of a new option for a life of
religious obedience: celibacy. It had been clearly stated by St Paul
that, in view of the approaching crisis (as he saw it), the freedom of
the single state was to be preferred to the domestic encumbrances

that go with married life. This suggested that in the longer term a celibate life might be a particularly appropriate and effective form of Christian self-dedication: had it not been authorized by Jesus' saying on 'making oneself a eunuch'? From this (among other factors) sprang the long history of Christian monasticism, in which a vow of celibacy was always essential. In due course celibacy was extended also to the priesthood of the Western church, and remains a condition of ordination in the Roman Catholic church to this day.

All this may or may not have been a correct inference from Jesus' teaching; but in any case it is unlikely to have been the point he was making here. We have seen that he used a startling example; and when he did this, it was usually to give people a jolt out of their normal, comfortable assumptions. What assumption could he have been attacking here? Presumably the social convention that everyone ought to get married. He is saying: what happens if you can't? And even if you can, might there be a good reason for not doing so?

For a moral and religious teacher, these questions were (so far as we know) unprecedented. And for good reason: if society has a norm (everyone should get married) and if this is believed to be God's will ('male and female he created them'), then it is inevitable that little respect should be paid to those who, for whatever reason, do not conform. Those who were physically incapable were treated as inferior to full citizens. Those women who failed to find a husband were mocked or pitied. Those who were widowed (of whom there were always many) were dependent on charity. Jesus chose the most offensive of the words that described any of these categories ('eunuch') and declared that it was a state that could be deliberately chosen for the sake of the kingdom. By implication, he restored dignity and respect to them all. The startling character of his language reinforced his startling conclusion: incapacity for marriage, or free renunciation of marriage, may offer an honourable passport to the kingdom of heaven.

In his time, the main thrust of this may have been to restore dignity to the single state. As such, it is likely to have been socially revolutionary and an innovation in religious thought; yet it is entirely of a piece with Jesus' other teaching, which again and again points to good practice and high personal qualities in the most unexpected people (such as Samaritans, or the very poor) and startles the respectable by showing up their complacency. In this case, Jesus may well have wanted to jolt people into realizing that those who were unmarried were suffering a social injustice; and in the subsequent history of Christianity this has had a powerful influence in securing respect for the 'vocation' which may be fulfilled by a single person (whether or not in a monastery). It could even be said that this respect for the single state is one of the most important contributions made by Jesus to human dignity and human rights.

(Incidentally, the church needs to be careful not to smother this insight by placing an exclusive emphasis on 'the family'. 'Family Services', with large numbers of children taking part, may be an excellent thing. But some church members are not married and may feel inferior; others who are married have no children and wish they had. If the norm for church services becomes something for parents and children, those who cannot be parents may feel devalued or excluded. This aspect of Jesus' teaching has not lost its relevance today, in the church as in the world.)

But there is one form of inability to be married which was not recognized as such in Jesus' time. Can his teaching apply to this also? I mentioned earlier that homosexuality was officially quite unacceptable in Jewish society. Homosexual acts were forbidden by law (Lev. 18.22; 20.13), and homosexual attachments were regarded as a 'perversion', alterable at will, and therefore sinful. This was the view inherited by Jesus, and there is no reason why he should have held any other. But today we believe we have evidence that in many cases sexual orientation is a natural attribute. People are lesbian or gay, not by choice or inclination, but because they are made that way. Some of them must be recognized as belonging to the class of those who *cannot* marry. If Jesus had known this, would he have used the same argument to promote respect for them as he did for 'eunuchs'?

The difficulty here, of course, is that what the Bible says about homosexuality seems to be so negative that it is difficult to see how it can be used to support anything but an outright condemnation. It is true that the Hebrew scriptures are not absolutely clear on the subject. Homosexual acts were certainly illegal, but this may not have been the real sin of the city of Sodom. In Genesis 19, what seems to have happened in Sodom is a homosexual rape, but the point of the story has more to do with a breach of the law of hospitality than with sexual immorality. In the prophets,[2] again, Sodom is certainly seen as a guilty city but its sins are apparently not confined to

---

[2] Jer. 23.14; Ezek. 16.49 etc.

homosexuality. It is only later that Sodom became a byword for just one type of sin. But there is no doubt that from quite an early date the culture was strongly opposed to homosexual practices, in part, perhaps, because of their association with pagan religions from which the Hebrews needed to distance themselves in every possible way. When we come to the New Testament the same attitude prevailed, and is most eloquently expressed by Paul in the first chapter of Romans. But by this time there was another factor. The alien culture from which the Jewish people was under the greatest pressure was no longer that of primitive Canaanite religions but of the highly sophisticated Graeco-Roman empire. Since the third century BC the Jews had struggled to preserve intact their own way of life, their religion and their morals against the insidious cultural influences that went with the use of the Greek language, the spread of Greek ideas and literature, and the establishment of Greek forms of administration and justice. Against all this, it seemed that their one protection was the moral and legal code embodied in the Law of Moses and the religious observances which effectively held the Jewish community together. From this vantage point a Jewish thinker would survey the pagan world around him and note those characteristics of its cosmopolitan civilization which were most threatening to Jewish identity and traditional Jewish practice. Most important of these was idolatry, symbolized by the innumerable statues of gods that were set up in public places throughout the empire. The Jewish religion firmly forbade all representations of the deity; the profusion of images purporting to be gods was a constant affront to their religious sensibility. The second feature of pagan life which caused alarm was its apparent immorality, represented in this case by the open acceptance of sexual practices that were abhorrent to Jewish ways, and from which only a strict adherence to the traditional attitudes entrenched in the Law of Moses could (it seemed) save them.

This is the setting for Paul's tirade against pagan civilization in the first chapter of Romans. He writes, of course, as a Christian. But at this point his thinking and reflexes are entirely Jewish. After a general attack on what we would now call the 'secular' climate of Greek thought (vv. 18–21) he identifies two main areas of pagan immorality which are exactly those of the standard Jewish polemic: idolatry and sexual misconduct. In the latter, he specifies what he is referring to: 'women have exchanged natural intercourse for unnatural . . . males behave indecently with males' (vv. 26–7). He takes for granted, like any Jewish thinker of his time, that such conduct is immoral; but he also uses the word 'nature' more than once, which suggests that, like other Jewish writers, he was familiar with the argument sometimes used by Stoic philosophers that homosexual acts were 'unnatural' (v. 26). This argument presupposes, of course, that everyone is 'by nature' heterosexual and that homosexuality is therefore 'perversion'.

There is no other passage in the New Testament where so much attention is paid to this issue, and there are only two other places where it is mentioned at all. In both of these it occurs simply in a list of immoral forms of behaviour.[3] Whether it is there because the Christian community actually needed to be warned against it we cannot be sure: it may simply be because it was almost instinctive to include the typically pagan sins of idolatry and sexual immorality in any list of vices. In any case, in any community of which the moral tone was predominantly Jewish (as was the case with most of the early churches) homosexual behaviour would have been socially unacceptable, and for that reason, once again, we should not be surprised if the New Testament does not say much about it. Where it does so, it is mainly in the context of a more or less conventional attack on pagan moral standards.

None of this implies, of course, that there is anything uncertain or provisional about the evidence in the Bible. Its condemnation of homosexual acts and inclinations is clear and forceful. All that this discussion has shown so far is that the strong language used about it must be seen in the context of the particular cultural and religious threats to which the Jews were exposed at the time. And for many readers of the Bible this may seem to settle the question. If scripture says something is wrong, wrong it must be. But can it ever be as simple as that? There are moral rules in the Old Testament which we believe to have been corrected in the New – the necessity of circumcision, the sabbath regulations, the easy permission for divorce. There are moral and social assumptions in both, which subsequent Christian thinking has revised – the acceptance of slavery, for instance or the subordination of women to men. In view of an increasing moral consensus around us that lesbians and gay men have 'rights', can we be sure that there is not another assumption here that ought to be corrected in the light of modern social conditions?

[3] I Cor. 6.9; I Tim. 1.10. 'Perverts' (REB) in Rev. 22.15 is an unlikely translation

To this, many will answer that, whatever may be the case in a matter of social organization and justice, sexual morality is different. Here, if anywhere, surely we can say that human nature does not change: what was wrong in the eyes of inspired biblical writers two thousand or more years ago must still be wrong today. Nevertheless it can hardly be denied that in this particular instance something *has* changed. Human nature may be the same; but our understanding of it is different. The phenomenon that some human beings may be attracted by members of their own sex and unable to form a relationship with members of the other sex is something which is capable of investigation in the light of modern biological, medical and psychological knowledge. Its causes may not yet have been established: we are still at the stage of theories rather than accepted explanations. Whether a person is born homosexual or caused to be so by early upbringing or influenced to be so in adolescence is still not known. But the question has now to be seen in the light of a well established understanding of human sexuality in general which was certainly not available when any part of the Bible was written. We now know that, for this purpose, it is not sufficient to think of human beings as either male or female. Just as it has always been obvious that some men have feminine characteristics and some women masculine ones, so now it is realized that all of us have both male and female components in our nature, and each one of us occupies a particular place on a spectrum which extends from almost exclusive masculinity to almost exclusive femininity. For most, the weight is strongly on one side or the other and manifests itself in an attraction for someone of the other sex; for some, there seems to be a more even balance, so that they are attracted by both sexes; for others again their sexuality seems to make them able to respond only to homophile relationships. To some degree these 'natural' variations may be subject to the will of the individual and to direction by social pressures and conventions. In others the sexual orientation is a fact of life and cannot be changed or wished away.

To accept that this is so is not to opt for one particular scientific theory which may be proved wrong tomorrow. It is to recognize the fundamental understanding on which all study of the human person will be based in the foreseeable future. Nor is it merely theoretical. There are many homosexuals who genuinely wish that they could become 'normal' and make great efforts to do so but find that it is quite beyond their power. It is no longer fair to them to suppose, in the face of an impressive scientific consensus to the contrary, that they could change simply by an exercise of the will: they know by painful experience that this is not so. But at the same time the scientific model of human sexuality as a spectrum on which each of us may have a slightly different place allows us to think that there are cases where the older view may not be altogether wrong. Where there is a clear orientation one way or the other there may be nothing the individual can do to change it, and it is inappropriate to use the language of moral choices. It is a condition that simply has to be lived with, and there can be no question of it being 'sinful'. But there may be points on the spectrum where a person is not fully determined one way or the other, and where it is possible to exercise the will and make a deliberate choice. If so, then the outcome may properly be subject to moral questioning, and judgments found in the Bible or in traditional Christian teaching may still be relevant.

The question, in other words, is not a simple one. Even the new understanding of human sexuality given by modern research does not allow us to say that a homosexual orientation is always 'natural' and never blameworthy. On the other hand it does allow us to say that it cannot always be, and is unlikely often to be, something that can be changed by the will and therefore open to moral judgment. And this brings us back to the saying of Jesus about eunuchs. Whether or not being sexually disabled or impotent was regarded as someone's 'fault', the sufferer tended to be socially shunned or excluded from society altogether. It was characteristic of Jesus to draw attention to this, and to restore dignity to such people by teaching that, far from being something to be despised, their condition could be voluntarily taken upon oneself 'for the sake of the kingdom'. Should not the same apply to homosexuals today? For too long they have been shunned and despised for something which many of them could not help. It would be in the spirit of Jesus' teaching to say that they too deserve not only respect and dignity but the opportunity to serve in God's kingdom.

To a certain extent the point has been taken in traditional Christian teaching. Men and women who have been unable to form a relationship with someone of the opposite sex have been offered an honoured place in celibate religious communities and generations of priests have found it possible to 'sublimate' their sexual energy in a life committed to celibacy and the loving service of all who were placed in their care. Of course there will have been countless cases of agonized struggle. Of course there will have been failures. But it would be unfair to the lives of a great many good people not to acknowledge the strength of their witness to a way of life that turned the renunciation of their sexuality into a deeply satisfying and loving relationship with a wide circle of fellow human beings, and in many cases liberated them for a life of sustained worship, service and prayer.

But there was a cost, not just in terms of the inner struggle and discipline involved, but of the burden borne by those for whom there was little possibility of such 'sublimation' and who may have lived lives of intense loneliness and frustration. There was always scope for applying the principle of Jesus' eunuch-saying. The challenge was always there to give such people honour and respect and to help them to find their opportunity for service. And now there is a new factor. When sexual intercourse was regarded as being primarily for the procreation of children, there could have been no question of it having a proper place in homosexual relationships: it was bound to appear 'unnatural'. But for some years now (as we saw in the chapter on marriage) the church has been teaching that 'bodily union' can 'strengthen the union of their hearts and lives'. Why should this apply only to heterosexuals? Should it not be equally true of gay and lesbian couples? Should not a recognition of their rightful place in society imply also endorsement of their right to physical intimacy when they form a lasting and loving relationship with someone of their own sex?

At this point we can no longer work with Jesus' saying on eunuchs. It would be absurd to use a saying that is to do with voluntary sexual renunciation 'for the sake of the kingdom' as an argument for approving of sexual intimacy in gay and lesbian relationships. But the principle we gained from that saying was that those who through no fault of their own cannot conform to the social norm of marriage deserve respect and dignity; and alongside that we must now place the further principle, implicit in the Bible and now explicit in much recent Christian teaching, that the union of hearts and minds can be strengthened by the union of bodies. If therefore two persons of the same sex have formed a deep emotional attachment, have 'consented' together in the sense that their relationship has been freely entered into on both sides, and from their knowledge of themselves and of one another can honestly say that they are committed to each other for life, it is difficult to see why they should not give physical expression to their love.

There is of course another factor to consider. Just as every marriage has a public and social aspect, so does every long-term homosexual relationship. Everyone is part of some community. Often these communities are self-selected: people may be more attached to a community created by work, sport or hobbies than to one that arises simply from where they happen to live. Gay and lesbian people will naturally make their friendships among others like themselves, and will feel that their relationships are fully accepted within their own 'community'. But the situation is different for Christians, each of whom is by the very fact of being a Christian integrated into a much more varied and representative community. As in society at large, the majority will be heterosexual. Many of these may have difficulty in acknowledging homosexuality. Some may still find it actually abhorrent. Members of a parish may learn to express their solidarity with a gay or lesbian couple just as they do with a newly-married couple. But for some it may still be extremely difficult.

This is one of the reasons for which the bishops of the Church of England have come to the conclusion (which is by no means universally accepted in the church) that clergy 'cannot claim the liberty to enter into sexually active homophile relationships'.[4] Ordained men and women have a public responsibility in their domestic lives. They have promised to 'fashion their own life and that of their household according to the way of Christ'.[5] In a parish or any social community where the majority regard marriage as the norm, an intimate sexual relationship other than marriage may be hard to accept in one whom they regard as placed among them to set an example of following 'the way of Christ'. But this can change. Thirty years ago British church congregations were disgracefully unprepared to accept black people as fellow Christians, with the result that great numbers felt hurt and rejected and resorted to new black churches. Today the evil of racism is more generally seen for what it is: most congregations have overcome their hostility (it was nothing less), many have become positively welcoming, and a few are now ministered to by black clergy. Similarly, until twenty years or so ago most bishops refused to ordain clergy who had been divorced, or who had married a divorcee, on the grounds that such a

---

[4] *Issues in Human Sexuality*, 1991, 5.17
[5] *Alternative Services Book 1980*, p.358

person could not give a 'wholesome example' (as the Book of Common prayer puts it) of family life to the parish. But again, parishes have changed, and many are now ready to accept such a minister if the second marriage appears to be secure. We may expect the same development to occur in the case of homosexual partnerships. Church communities do not move faster than the society they live in, though they may sometimes succeed in taking the lead. It may not yet be possible for most of them to accept that a priest who has a gay or lesbian partner can set an example that will be helpful to the majority of Christian homes; but many may come to recognize that what such a partnership can do for other homosexuals living in the parish and conscientiously working out their own pattern of domestic life may outweigh the disadvantages of not having a conventional family in the vicarage.

The bishops used the phrase, 'claim the liberty'. This is the language of rights, which is the language in which much of the debate about the social acceptance of homosexuality has been conducted in recent years. Should the 'age of consent' for homosexual males remain at twenty-one when for heterosexuals it is sixteen? Should homosexuality be a bar to some professions? Should a permanent homosexual partnership receive less social acceptance than marriage? Should marriage itself be reserved for 'this man and this woman'? These questions are naturally and properly debated in terms of rights. Once it is granted that homosexuality is a 'natural' condition, then any practical disadvantage or derogatory label which society attaches to it becomes something which must be fought against in the name of the rights which should be possessed by all. At the very heart of the moral consensus which now surrounds the concept of human rights is a protest against any form of discrimination carried out against people on grounds of race, colour, gender or religion – that is, on grounds of some characteristic which one is either born with or has come to hold as a matter of conscience and belief. Homosexuals surely belong to this category, and still suffer some forms of discrimination. It is a clear Christian duty to promote their rights.

But with rights go responsibilities. There is the responsibility, first, for preserving respect for the sexual act. Christians do not believe that merely because contraception has reduced the importance of procreation in sexual activity there is any less necessity to confine it to a totally committed relationship. Similarly with homosexuals: the

fact that it will necessarily be non-procreative does not mean that
it can be pursued merely for pleasure or as an adjunct to a casual
relationship. If its real purpose is 'to strengthen the union of
hearts and lives', then it is a perversion of it to use it for anything
less. Homosexuals have a responsibility to witness to this understanding of sex just as much as heterosexuals. Indeed they can
strengthen the witness of the church to this fundamental understanding of the deep significance of sexuality over against the
trivialization of sex and its commercial exploitation which are
blunting the sensibility and cheapening the personal aspirations of
so many people today.

There is the responsibility, secondly, to settle for nothing less than
lifelong relationships. There is no reason to expect a homophile
partnership to be easier than a married one – indeed it is often said
that until there is a greater degree of social acceptance the pressures
such partnerships are exposed to greatly reduce their chances of
success. Be that as it may, there is the same responsibility as for those
intending to get married, not just to make sure that there is
absolutely free consent on both sides, but for the partners to discover
whether they can realistically look forward to spending the whole of
their lives together. With the right of homosexuals to a public
partnership goes the responsibility, which they share with married
couples, to commit themselves publicly and unreservedly to lifelong
fidelity.

There is a third responsibility of a slightly different kind. I have
argued that it is not just a Christian conviction, it is for the good of
society itself, that children should be brought up so far as possible in
the security of the home of their two natural parents. If this is so, then
the responsibility for protecting such homes falls, not only on those
who may become parents themselves, but also on those who do not
or cannot. Some people appear to be genuinely bisexual, that is, they
are attracted by members of either sex. Since the argument for the
respect and dignity that are due to homosexuals is based on the fact
that they *cannot* form heterosexual relationships, then clearly the
same argument will not do for bisexuals. On the contrary, their
prime duty is to express their sexuality in a relationship which can
develop into parenthood; if they can do this, any homophile
relationship will be dangerous, if not destructive, for their family, or
at least lead them away from their responsibility to society.

But the same responsibility extends to homosexuals. There is said to be evidence that there are some young people whose sexual orientation does not become determined until well after adolescence and who are open to influence one way or the other. So long as it remains possible that they may happily marry and have a family, there is a responsibility laid on all of us to help them to find their sexual identity in this way. Homosexuals have a right to be honoured as what they are – so long as they can do no other. But this does not imply the right to influence in the same direction others (particularly adolescents) who may be free to opt otherwise. If we all have a responsibility to maintain a society in which the norm is for children to be brought up by their natural parents, none of us has the right actively to promote a different pattern among those who are capable of natural parenting. Every interest group is required to think of what is good for society as well as good for themselves. Here also rights carry responsibilities. Just as it is reasonable to expect gay and lesbian people to observe the same degree of decency in public places as heterosexual couples, so they can be expected to support, and not undermine, those patterns of behaviour and family institutions which, even if not open to themselves, are essential for the well-being of society.

For church members, all this can be put in a much more positive way. The church is a community of which, by definition, everyone may be a member. There is no race, gender, colour or disability of any kind which disqualifies. Every human being is equally a child of God. But this community has the task of witnessing to a distinctive way of life. So far as sex is concerned, it has a clear message. Sexual intercourse has its place in a totally committed, loving and exclusive relationship, in which the partners pledge their mutual fidelity for life. Any trivialization of sex, its use for casual gratification or commercial gain, is to be vigorously resisted. In this, all church members have a part. For some this will mean deliberate restraint followed by a genuine commitment leading to marriage. For some it will mean voluntary renunciation and abstinence. For some disabled people it may mean finding other ways of expressing and receiving love. For homosexuals it will mean that their partnership and the physical expression they give to their love become a means by which they too can promote the Christian understanding of sex as a seal and a strengthening of a lifelong relationship. Any of us may fail; but all are partners in the same aspiration, the same task. Whether by voluntary abstinence, disciplined restraint or proper enjoyment, or even as disabled or incapacitated, it is for us to witness to the rewards and the sheer goodness which flow from this God-given means of deepening and enriching a lifelong relationship of mutual and disinterested love.

9

Remorse and Renewal

'The Church of England affirms . . . that marriage is in its nature a union permanent and lifelong . . . ' This statement of Canon Law[1] sounds clear and definite. It appeals for its authority to 'our Lord's teaching' and it is faithfully reflected in the marriage service of the church. Yet today anyone who makes this statement may be accused of not facing the facts. One in three marriages are *not* lifelong, and the church itself is often ready to authorize a second marriage when the first partner is still alive. Even the belief that 'our Lord's teaching' unequivocally supports the doctrine that marriage must *always* be lifelong is (I have argued) open to question. So can the church continue to 'affirm' its traditional doctrine in such uncompromising terms? Can Christians still claim to hold this belief and witness to it in the lives of themselves and their families without resorting to humbug and pretence?

In one sense the question is not new. The church has always had a double task: to demand an absolute standard of marriage and family life from its members, but at the same time to care for those whose marriages fail. If it insists too rigorously on the absolute standard by shunning those who fail to reach it, it can be criticized for its lack of care for those who are most in need of help and support; if it seeks to include these casualties within its caring community it is criticized for relaxing its absolute standard of lifelong marriage. If it tries to avoid both these dangers it will be accused of hypocrisy and pretence. The mere fact of having both a high ideal to proclaim and a pastoral concern for those who cannot achieve it has always placed the church in a predicament, which can be resolved only by relaxing its demands (which would be faithless) or by shutting its doors to those who cannot conform (which would be uncaring). The fact that it cannot speak out with complete clarity need not be a sign of

[1] *The Canons of the Church of England*, 1969, B30

pretence or hypocrisy. It is the inevitable result of trying to do two things at once: to witness to the Christian understanding of marriage as a lifelong union and to hold within its fellowship those whose marriages have broken down.

This said, however, there is more than one way in which the church can cope with this inevitable tension. It can continue to proclaim that every marriage is for life and that divorce and remarriage are forbidden, and can solemnly warn those who are married in church of the consequences of settling for anything less. It can still show concern for those whose marriages have failed, but it cannot allow them full rights and true respect in the church community for fear of compromising the rule. In other words, this way involves an element of pretence – the pretence that the church cares for its casualties even though it cannot give them even the welcome it gives to those who have failed or sinned in other ways. Unfortunately, this is the way in which many ministers and congregations feel bound to handle the matter. Any more overt reception of divorced people would, they believe, compromise their efforts to maintain the Christian standard of lifelong marriage; yet they recognize that many of those who have entered on a second marriage may in other respects be setting a much more 'Christian' example of family life than some who are struggling with their first, and may have a faith which deserves full recognition and pastoral care. This response to the inevitable tension between upholding a standard and caring for those who fail results in more and more unhappiness as the number of divorces continues to rise.

There is, however, another way of showing seriousness about the lifelong character of marriage than by just proclaiming it as a rule. I have been arguing that many things about marriage today are different from what they were. Many of the constraints which used to hold families together – the economic dependence of the wife on the husband, the mutual interest of parents and children in each other's welfare – have diminished or disappeared, in some cases to the benefit of all. The growing equality of opportunities for both partners, the longer expectation of life, the smaller proportion of time devoted to child-rearing, the lack of support from an extended family – all these are factors which make the project of sharing one's whole life with another both more challenging and more rewarding. It is a project in which an increasing number of people find they fail, at least in the first attempt. It may not be particularly helpful to them if the church simply reiterates that they cannot officially be allowed a second chance. Would not a more positive approach be to suggest what resources there are – in themselves, in their community and in their faith – to help people fulfil the promise they still readily make to stay together until parted by death?

These resources are both personal and social. There is, first, the capacity to forgive and be forgiven. 'Forgive us our trespasses, as we forgive those who trespass against us.' This is a fundamental principle, vigorously insisted on by Jesus, but often misunderstood. Because it occurs in a prayer, and belongs to religion, it is easily thought of as a private transaction between me and God: if I forgive the person who offends me (which I can do simply by making up my mind not to bear a grudge), I can be confident that God will forgive me any wrong I have done to others. The whole process takes place in the privacy of my mind. But if I have offended some person, it is not enough for me to make a private confession and believe that God forgives me. God cannot settle things between me and another human being. It is the other person, not just God, to whom I have to go and be ready to make amends. Only then can I receive the forgiveness from a fellow human being which makes God's forgiveness possible. Jesus puts the matter with absolute directness.

> If you are presenting your gift at the altar and suddenly remember that your brother has a grievance against you, leave your gift where it is before the altar. First go and make your peace with your brother; then come back and offer your gift (Matt. 5. 23–24).

In other words, it is no use going to God for forgiveness if we have not gone to our fellow human beings for forgiveness first. It is all too easy to concentrate on the second half of the clause in the Lord's Prayer: God will forgive me so long as I am forgiving. But in the first half we ask to be forgiven *our* offences; and this cannot happen until we have made it up with the person we have offended.

This is not just piety: it is sound psychology. No close relationship with another human being is possible without constant offence being given and taken. On each occasion, if one is the offender, one's instinctive next move is to try to justify oneself – 'Well, wouldn't *you* have been angry?', and so forth. Less natural (and therefore often embarrassing) but infinitely more creative and healing is confessing one's fault and asking to be forgiven. If the partner can respond with genuine forgiveness (which may be equally costly) the episode can be one of many that will deepen and strengthen their partnership. This is no more than common sense. But it goes against the grain. Admitting one is wrong is usually the last thing one wants to do. 'Stick to your guns', 'stand up to him', 'don't let her get you down' – these are the slogans by which we are taught to keep up our self-confidence. At an early stage in a loving relationship they may be forgotten. All that lovers want to do is to lose themselves in each other, not justify themselves against each other. But in due course the old instincts re-emerge, and it is then that religion offers precious resources. Confessing and being forgiven can be brought out of the religious compartment of one's life (where they are so easily thought of as a private and 'spiritual' transaction between God and oneself) and applied to the obstinate realities of married life. Then, through the experience of being forgiven by a loving and beloved human partner, one may begin to understand what it is to be forgiven by God – which is something everyone is taught to pray for from earliest years. Forgiving and being forgiven become, not an embarrassment or a penance, but a liberation from instinctive slogans into a realm of increasing freedom and love.

Secondly, Christianity has something important to say about love. We saw how St Paul wrote of it. 'Love is patient and kind . . . never quick to take offence . . . keeps no score of wrongs', and so forth. We saw how Jesus told us to love even our enemies. We can see how such love could heal most of the scars of married life. But is it within our reach? It looks as if both Paul and Jesus were setting a standard that is beyond us. But I have already given examples of the way in which Jesus characteristically gave his moral teaching. He did not offer an ideal that no human being could ever have measured up to. On the contrary: he pointed to instances (sometimes in the most unexpected places – among Samaritans, among lazy neighbours, among arbitrary employers) where people do actually perform actions of astonishing goodness and generosity. And his message was then startlingly simple: why don't you do the same yourselves? And so with love. All of us have seen couples (not necessarily Christians) who are capable of the most splendid self-giving. It is not beyond our capacity: why don't we do the same? But in this case there is something more. When a relationship begins with passionate love, such loving conduct is no problem. Later, the passion may cool, and give place to something more prosaic. But the partners can never say that such all-enduring, disinterested love is beyond them. They have already given and received it themselves. All they have to do is go on with it – though now it is a matter, not so much of the feelings, as of the will. And strengthening the will – through instruction, through discouraging self-pretence, through holding before us a vision of what we might and long to be – is the business of religion.

But the resources are also social. As the project of marriage becomes more risk-laden and demanding, the need for community support becomes ever greater. Secular society today has little to offer in this respect. The stress laid on individual independence and freedom of choice has left little space for the kind of community solidarity that is required for marriages to flourish. Yet this is precisely what the church should be able to offer. To some extent it does so, through organizations like the Mother's Union (which is international) and the Children's Society (which works in England and Wales). But until recently the Mother's Union found itself in the predicament which has so often been that of the church itself: it continued to proclaim traditional standards of married and family life at a time when a growing number of people no longer conformed to them. In particular, anyone who was divorced was excluded in order that its members could give an unambiguous example of Christian family life. This has now changed: qualifications for membership have been relaxed, and prominent Mother's Union personalities have publicly refused to condemn new forms of family life. It still has the drawback (at least in this country) of its name. Though many men, and some families, are now members, it is perhaps difficult for the public at large to think of it as not just for mothers but for any parents or married persons, just as many people will be unaware that the Children's Society (which began in the nineteenth century as 'Waifs and Strays') is a resource for parents and families as well as for children and young people. But organizations of this kind are of critical importance. Not only should they be represented in every parish: every parish should aim to *be* such a society, in which all those who have taken upon themselves the challenge of sexual restraint, marital fidelity and family priorities should support and help each other through the various phases of married and family life.

We use a number of metaphors to describe a marriage that is getting into difficulties. We say that it is 'under strain', is 'breaking up' (presumably the image is that of a frozen pond, no longer safe to walk on), has 'broken down' (like a car) or (finally) that it is 'dead'.

These metaphors are significant. They suggest that there is something called 'a marriage' out there, independent of the parties whose
marriage it is, and that things can happen to this marriage which are
not directly caused by either of them. This way of speaking now finds
support in the law. Until recently, obtaining a divorce meant proving
a 'matrimonial offence': one of the parties must be shown to have
behaved in such a way (usually adultery or cruelty) as to make it
reasonable for the court to grant a divorce to the injured party. The
breakdown of a marriage, in other words, was the fault of either the
husband or the wife; and the purpose of legal proceedings was to
establish whether the accused party was 'guilty'. There are, of
course, many cases where this approach is appropriate. When a
husband goes off with another woman, leaving his devoted wife to
cope with his children and all the domestic consequences of his
desertion, it makes good sense to say that he is guilty of an offence
and that his wife should have some remedy at law. But suppose the
immediately preceding years had been telling a different story.
Suppose she had become a difficult and excessively demanding wife,
no longer responding to his love and jealous of his influence on his
own children; suppose that her tempers and her intransigence had
begun to make their married life virtually insupportable. In such a
case, what sense is there in looking for 'the guilty party'? How could
there be just one 'matrimonial offence' of adultery? Clearly both
parties were at fault; and it was hardly a good use of expensive legal
proceedings to try to determine which of them was the more to
blame. Surely what the court had to do was not to identify the
'offender' but to judge whether circumstances were now such that
husband and wife should be released from their marriage. It would
remain only to arrive at a just decision with regard to their conflicting
claims to their children (if they had any) and their property.

Such was the thinking that led to the Divorce Reform Act of 1969.
Under this Act, for the first time, the legal ground for divorce became
the 'irretrievable breakdown' of a marriage. It was no longer
necessary to identify one of the parties as the 'offender'. It was the
marriage itself that was now under judgment. If this had effectively
'died', a court could properly dissolve it. Whose 'fault' it was was no
one's business but the couple's themselves. This legislation was of
course resisted at the time because it was feared that it would make
divorce easier. Certainly the divorce rate has risen sharply since that
date, and there was an initial surge of cases as soon as the Act came

into effect: couples unable or unwilling to prove an 'offence' against each other at last saw a prospect of release from what had become an unendurable situation. But the reasoning behind the change was widely seen to be sensible and humane. Indeed the Church of England itself had published an official and carefully researched study[2] recommending that the law should be reformed in this direction. No one wished to see the divorce rate rise, no one wished divorce to be available simply because husband and wife decided not to go on with their marriage. But all agreed that there were countless occasions when it makes little sense to ask who is 'guilty'. What the courts need to reach a judgment on is not the 'offence' of one of the parties but the state of the marriage itself.

But out of this change has arisen something which was certainly not intended at the time: the concept of 'no fault' divorce, a concept which may well lead to further legislation along the lines of enabling a couple to divorce after a relatively short period of apparent failure. When the Church of England, along with many experienced and compassionate people, proposed that divorce should not require establishing a 'matrimonial offence', they did not for one moment suggest that a divorce is no one's 'fault'. On the contrary, any failure of marriage is like to be both parties' fault: and the point at issue was whether it was a good use of a court's time (and did anything but damage to the parties themselves) to try to establish which of them was the more to blame. The danger of changing the law along those lines was not so much that it would encourage people to divorce (the rise in the divorce rate is due to many more factors than this) as that, by shifting attention from the offence of an individual to the breakdown of a marriage, it would allow the parties to feel less responsible for failure: it was the marriage that had broken down, not one (or both) of them who had done wrong. It seemed as if there was no longer any need to talk about 'fault'.

It is here that the Christian religion really does have something to say. If there is any pretence involved, this time it is not in the church, it is in anyone who suggests that divorce is nobody's fault. There is no such thing as a marriage without a husband and wife who have freely given their consent to one another. There is no such thing as a marriage breakdown without each of them having contributed their share of intolerance, selfishness or faithlessness. For either to say

[2] *Putting Asunder – A Divorce Law for Contemporary Society*, 1966

they are not at fault is sheer self-deception. Of course one may be much more so than the other, but both are to blame, neither can shuffle off responsibility.

There is a clear difference here between the judgment of the world and the judgment of Christians. In the world, as in the law, when some offence is committed the important thing is to find the offender. Once he or she is found and convicted, the offence is, so to speak, purged; everyone else is by implication innocent. English law works with just two possible verdicts, 'guilty' and 'not guilty'. Similarly, society instinctively looks for a criminal or a scapegoat when anything goes wrong. Once such a person is found and receives appropriate blame or punishment, no one else is required to carry responsibility. It is of course often realized that this may not be the whole story. Scottish law reflects the complexity of human wrong-doing more accurately: besides the verdicts of guilty and not guilty it has a third, 'innocent', reserved for the relatively rare cases when the accused is shown to have had nothing whatever to do with the crime. 'Not guilty', after all, means only that the evidence is not strong enough to secure conviction: few of those who are acquitted of criminal charges are blameless in every respect. 'Innocence' is a rare condition, at least among adults.

It is this general lack of innocence that Christianity takes seriously with its doctrine of sin. Of course some people are much more wicked than others, but even the least wicked are not altogether good. In the eyes of God we are all way behind the line he has set for us to reach, and the difference between the relative sinfulness of myself and that of a convicted criminal is far less important than the difference between the sinfulness of us all and the goodness which God expects of us. For a religious person, to think otherwise involves pretence and self-deception. To recognize and acknowledge this is to distance oneself from the ethos of secular society, in which justifying oneself and showing oneself not to be at fault is not just instinctive but is actively encouraged.[3] In sheer psychological terms, this acknowledgment may often be a relief and start a healing process. In the Christian faith it is much more. It is a means of liberation from the weight of the past and of establishing a relationship, not just with others, but with God. It is the necessary preliminary for receiving

[3] Your insurers will not be pleased if you say 'my fault' at the scene of a road accident! 'Never admit responsibility' is an insidious motto that extends far beyond traffic offences

from God the power to become, despite ourselves, the human agents of his reconciling love.

It is therefore not just sound psychology, it is a fundamental Christian perception of what it is to be human, that makes us say that there can be no such thing as 'no fault divorce'. This does not mean that we should once again start looking for the guilty party in every broken marriage. It means that we must recognize that we are all at fault. When a marriage is under strain, indeed long before, there are many people who might have cared more than they did – relatives, friends, neighbours, church people, ministers of religion, counsellors – and offered help and support. The partners themselves had the opportunity to identify their own failures, to confess them and to receive forgiveness and strengthening from each other. Each will have offended the other in far more ways than they are conscious of and will have contributed in some measure to the tension which is threatening the marriage. Both must accept responsibility; and their best resource for healing the wound in their union is the repeated cycle of facing and acknowledging the reality about themselves, sincerely wishing and praying to be otherwise, receiving liberation from the sins of the past and embracing new possibilities for the future – all of which is at the heart of the practice of the Christian religion. Not only the partners themselves, but all those willing to bear some responsibility for their marriage, are in some sense 'at fault'. They need to bring to bear on it the resources of their faith that in all suffering and hurt, in all misunderstanding and tension, as in all sin confessed and forgiven, there are the seeds of new life and loving reconciliation.

But we must be realistic. The fact we are sinners means that there is no human enterprise in which we are bound to succeed. Christ may have told us what a marriage should be, but he certainly did not promise to equip us so that we could not fail. Failure, of one sort or another, is built into our humanity. There is no way that our marriages could have been exempt from it. But the whole story of Jesus, and (in a sense) of every Christian, is to do with failure, and with being taken through failure into a new quality of life. What has this to say about the particular failure which so many people experience today – the failure of their marriage?

Let us return to one of the metaphors used to describe the situation. We say that a marriage has 'died'. Once again we must not let this deceive us into thinking that something can happen to a

marriage independently of the two people who are married. There is
no entity called a marriage which can sicken and die without the
persons concerned being affected. And indeed this is the experience
of many whose marriages have come to an end. It is not some
external thing, it is something in themselves, that has 'died'. Sharing
one's life, one's feelings, one's inmost thoughts with another for any
length of time creates a bond that is not severed without pain. One
becomes, in subtle ways, a different person; one's life develops a
texture that is more complex, potentially more satisfying, but also
more vulnerable, than before. In this sense, as I said earlier, marriage
is indissoluble. A person develops in the married relationship in a
new way: changes take place that are irreversible. If it comes to an
end, the texture woven over months and years is brutally torn. There
is not just a radical disruption of home and family life, there is an end
of shared pleasures and responsibilities, carefully acquired habits
and skills become useless or irrelevant, the assurance of support and
understanding has disappeared, there is a deep sense of failure, a loss
of self-esteem. Divorce is tragic, not just for the children who are
notoriously the victims, but for the spouses who are left with
shattered dreams and torn personalities. If we speak of the 'death' of
a marriage, the same metaphor often fits those who were married:
something in them has 'died'.

But this metaphor, again, takes us to the heart of Christianity. If I
speak of death and resurrection as a 'metaphor', this does not mean
that I do not believe they are real. On the contrary, I believe that
resurrection is a reality so profound and mysterious that it cannot be
described directly. Metaphors are one of the resources we need for
talking about it. Consider these words of Jesus in John's Gospel:

> In very truth I tell you, if anyone obeys my teaching he will never
> see death (8.51).

In any literal sense this is plainly untrue. Not even the greatest of
Christian saints have been spared the biological necessity of death.
Christianity is not a magic potion offering a fairy-tale immortality to
those who take it correctly. Consequently Jesus' words must be
understood in a sense that may be called metaphorical. It is *as if* 'he
will never see death'. We must put this alongside another saying:

> God . . . gave his only son, so that everyone who has faith in him
> may not perish but have eternal life (3.16).

In John's Gospel both life and death serve as powerful metaphors. 'Life' is that quality of living which becomes possible through faith in Christ: it is 'eternal', in that it is not interrupted by physical death but continues in a form of closer communion with God. 'Death' is the absence of that quality, a refusal to accept the offer of 'life', as a result of which we bring judgment upon ourselves.

All this is just one way – the way of the Fourth Gospel – of finding words to express the new reality which came into the world with Christ's resurrection. St Paul had another way. For him, it was 'death' that said more as a metaphor even than 'life'. The resurrection had been preceded by Jesus' death – his real, physical death. There was nothing metaphorical about that. But if Christians were to share that resurrection life they too must undergo a kind of 'death'. Paul found this 'dying' in the experience of conversion: we 'die to sin', 'the old Adam dies in us', we 'die to the world'. An inner change takes place which is *like* death and is followed by new life. By such metaphors these early writers sought to convey the very essence of the Christian experience. The 'life' which Christ has made possible for us is preceded and prepared for by a kind of 'death'. Hence the paradoxical front which Christianity presents to the world: failure is more significant than success, weakness than strength. Suffering is given meaning by Christ's suffering; 'dying' enables us to travel with Christ through death to new life.

If, therefore, people whose marriage has ended in divorce speak of the experience as a kind of 'death', they are using a metaphor that has powerful Christian resonances. They use the word primarily, of course, to express the sheer pain of what they have been through and the sense of bereavement which they feel with the ending of a relationship that started out with such high hopes and expectations. But in the light of their Christian faith they may come to find that the metaphor leads into the building of a genuinely new life. Often this will be life in a second marriage with a new partner. But if they are encouraged to take the word 'death' seriously this will be far more than just confessing failure and trying again. It will mean coming to terms in as much honesty as one is capable of with one's responsibility for all that was wrong in the first marriage, and allowing God to perform his miracle of bestowing new and genuine life in the second. Sin, confession, forgiveness, renewal, is the authentic Christian rhythm in every other aspect of the moral life. Who dares deny that it may be heard also in the trauma of a failed marriage, sincerely acknowledged and graciously healed through the new life of a second love?

It is often said that a second marriage cannot take place in church while the first partner is alive because it would make nonsense of the marriage service. How can one seriously vow to be someone's wife or husband 'till death us do part' if there is another person around to whom one has made the same promise? One way round this would be to re-write the service for the occasion. One could use a form of words to suggest that having failed to keep one's word once one ought not to be absolutely trusted a second time. But, quite apart from the fact that this is not likely to be what is in anyone's mind at the time, the suggestion rests on a misunderstanding about vows. In an earlier chapter we looked at the philosophy of vows, and I argued that there may be circumstances in which a vow cannot be fulfilled and must be allowed to lapse. To this I would now want to add an argument based on Christian theology. Jesus certainly set us a high standard to aim at, in marriage as well as in other things. Indeed he went so far as to tell us to be 'perfect'. But he never spoke of human beings as if they could become proof against failure and sin. Even those closest to him and constantly under the influence of his teaching and his inspiration remained capable of conduct they had vowed to avoid: one betrayed him, one disowned him in public, and the rest deserted him at the moment of crisis. What Jesus looked for in men and women (and perhaps found particularly in children) was not a faultless record of good deeds and well-kept promises but a readiness to acknowledge faults and failures, to 'turn' in a new direction, to be forgiven and to begin life afresh in penitence and faith. There is no authority in his teaching for treating the breaking of a marriage vow as something exceptional that cannot be redeemed like any other sin. And the form which redemption takes may well be the raising of a new vow, a new absolute commitment, out of the ashes of the old.

I therefore do not see any reason either in philosophy or in theology for suggesting that the vows taken by a divorced person should be in some way less whole-hearted, less unconditional than those prescribed in the present marriage service. Indeed it would be odd if the commitment made in church were to be less absolute than that made in a registry office (where every certified marriage is 'for life'). And in any case such a policy would be extremely unhelpful to the couple themselves, whose determination to stay together might be all the stronger in the light of the previous unhappy experience. This part of the marriage service surely ought to be the same whether or not one or both of those being married has a partner still living. But this does not mean that the entire procedure should be exactly the same a second time. We do not want the church to be rescued from the pretence that it can never solemnize a second marriage only to fall into the new pretence that it is as if there had been no previous marriage. The strongest ground for authorizing remarriage is, in the end, theological: the opportunity it gives to enter into the mystery of the death and resurrection of Christ through dying to one marriage and finding new life in a second. This is a process that involves effort and pain, self-knowledge and repentance, liberation and renewal. It is something that the couple who are now to share everything between them must have been able to work through together. Their past is something in which there is no room for pretence; it must be fully confessed and forgiven lest it returns to haunt them later on. It is the task and the privilege of the Christian minister to help them through this essential preparation; and it is for the church to authorize forms of service, whether private or public, which will provide a focus for this vital part of the couple's preparation and an assurance that it has been sincerely attempted.

Sin, confession, forgiveness, renewal: this, the basic rhythm of the Christian life, is the precious gift which the church has to offer the world. Moral standards and conventions may change, new possibilities and opportunities may cause a redrawing of moral boundaries. Simply recalling people to traditional moral rules is a defensive and usually unhelpful reaction. Not all those rules were soundly based; some have become inappropriate to modern conditions. What the church must proclaim is rather its understanding of sexuality and marriage in the light of Christian principles, of the goals that are set before us, and above all of the resources which God has given us for dealing lovingly and creatively with our inevitable failures.

To sum up: *Our understanding of sex* is that it has its place only in a fully committed relationship. This relationship, we now see, may begin before marriage, and if it looks forward to marriage it may be a proper context for sexually expressed love. Of course, the prevailing social attitude to sex is more permissive. Relatively few young people can be expected to have the maturity of faith and character which can take the place of the social constraints of a former age. We cannot blame them if the Christian insistence on sexual restraint has not yet influenced them as strongly as the wide-spread social acceptance of short-term sexual relationships. Later, as they come to experience absolute commitment to another person, and the place of sex within it, they may come to have regrets, and even a sense of shame and failure in the face of their partner. Christianity invites us to recognize such regrets not as a source of guilt, but as remorse for sin that can lead to reconciliation with God and with another person and sets us on a path of renewal and freedom.

Our understanding of marriage is that it is for life. But our focus is not on the institution, still less on the question whether a successful marriage is a necessary passport to the community of faith. Our focus is on those who become partners in the lifelong marriage project. In them we see human beings as Jesus saw them, subject to failure, disappointment, self-deception and complacency – in short, subject to sin. To them he gave the assurance that they could come to terms with themselves as they really are and grasp the new possibilities which God holds out to them. As married or as single people, as one of a heterosexual majority or a homosexual minority, as disabled or celibate, as men and women who succeed or fail in marriage as in everything else – all have the same message addressed to them, and the church's first priority must be to make it heard.

Jesus said (using a metaphor so strong that it is not for the squeamish): 'If your right eye causes your downfall, tear it out and fling it away' (Matt. 5.29). St Paul, using a different metaphor, gave this common-sense truth its theological dimension: 'If we thus died with Christ, we believe that we shall also live with him . . . you must regard yourselves as dead to sin and alive to God in union with Christ Jesus' (Rom. 6.8,11). We can extend Paul's metaphor to the whole range of experience touched on in this book. There is, for some, a dying of hope – hope for a particular love, or for ever being loved; for others, a dying to transient physical desire for the sake of its future fulfilment; for most of us, a dying to those preferences and prejudices, those obstinate relics of selfishness, that threaten every loving relationship; for divorcees, a dying when that relationship has to be abandoned; for all, a dying to the pretence which hides these realities from us and in which religion so often connives. To such dying is attached a promise – whether in love, in marriage and family, or indeed (for we have been touching its very heart) in our Christian faith – the promise of resurrection and new life.

Index